Black Girl in the Middle

To my precious daughters, Madison and Miah, you are the light in my life, the reason I continue to push forward. May you always walk in confidence, knowing that your voice, your presence, and your dreams matter.

And to every Black girl who has ever felt caught in the middle—between expectations and aspirations, between who the world says you should be and who you truly are—this is for you. May you always stand boldly in your truth, knowing that you are powerful, worthy, and enough.

Black Girl in the Middle

Five Transformative Practices to Make Schools Better for Black Girls

Melody Hawkins

CORWIN

FOR INFORMATION:

Corwin
A SAGE Company
2455 Teller Road
Thousand Oaks, California 91320
(800) 233-9936
www.corwin.com

SAGE Publications Ltd.
1 Oliver's Yard
55 City Road
London EC1Y 1SP
United Kingdom

SAGE Publications India Pvt. Ltd.
Unit No 323-333, Third Floor, F-Block
International Trade Tower Nehru Place
New Delhi 110 019
India

SAGE Publications Asia-Pacific Pte. Ltd.
18 Cross Street #10-10/11/12
China Square Central
Singapore 048423

Vice President and
  Editorial Director: Monica Eckman
Acquisitions Editor: Megan Bedell
Senior Content
  Development Editor: Mia Rodriguez
Content Development and
  Operations Manager: Lucas Schleicher
Senior Editorial
  Assistant: Natalie Delpino
Production Editor: Tori Mirsadjadi
Copy Editor: Colleen Brennan
Typesetter: C&M Digitals (P) Ltd.
Cover Designer: Gail Buschman
Marketing Manager: Melissa Duclos

Contents

Acknowledgments

First and foremost, I give all honor and glory to my Lord and Savior, Jesus Christ. Without His guidance, strength, and wisdom, this book would not exist. I find my purpose and unwavering belief in this work through Him. Every word I write, every effort to uplift and advocate for Black girls, is an extension of the calling He has placed on my life. Thank You, Lord, for ordering my steps, reminding me that I am never alone, and carrying me through every challenge. May this book reflect Your love for the girls and women who need to know they are seen, valued, and deeply loved.

Writing *Black Girl in the Middle* has been a journey of reflection, healing, and advocacy. This book exists because of the collective efforts of so many who have poured into me, supported me, and inspired me to keep going. It is an offering to those who stand in the middle—navigating expectations, confronting barriers, and daring to create space where none was freely given.

This book would not exist without the researchers, scholars, and advocates whose work illuminated Black girlhood's complexities and strengthened my understanding. In particular, the Georgetown Law Center on Poverty and Inequality's Initiative on Gender Justice and Opportunity—your research on adultification, discipline disparities, and how Black girls are denied grace and protection has been groundbreaking. Your scholarship affirms what so many of us have long known but struggled to prove. Thank you for your commitment to justice.

To the community leaders, activists, and organizations working to ensure Black girls receive the support, opportunities, and protection they deserve—your labor does not go unnoticed. Because of you, progress continues, and more Black girls thrive unapologetically.

To the educators who create spaces where Black girls feel seen and empowered—you are the heart of this work. I extend my deepest gratitude to Mrs. Ann Marshall and Mrs. Lydia Lane, whose stories are included in this book and who have worked closely with me to support Black girls, including my own. Mrs. Lane, for your intentionality and care in supporting not just the Black girls in your classroom but my daughter as well, thank you. Your impact is immeasurable.

To the teachers at Vine Middle School, where my teaching journey began—we knew the urgency of our work, and we did it. Against every odd, we never let up. We never stopped for our students. We cried, we rejoiced, we endured. We are victorious. You taught me what it means to stand in the gap, fight for equity, and love our students fiercely. Your lessons continue to shape the educator and advocate I am today.

To my mentors, peers, and fellow educators—your guidance and belief in my voice kept me moving forward, even when the work felt daunting.

To Alex Kajitani and Tom Rademacher—outside of my family, you were the first to hear about this book, and from day one, you encouraged me to keep writing, editing, and pushing forward. Your belief in this book before it even existed gave me the confidence to keep going. Tom, I will never forget your words: "Let's make a book!"

A special thank-you to Megan Bedell and the Corwin team for your commitment to bringing this book to life. Your patience, guidance, and dedication to ensuring this work reaches those who need it most have meant everything.

To my best friend and fellow educator, Charlie Edmonds—you never let me give up on this. Since we were two little Black girls in Jackson, Tennessee, you have been my sounding board, encourager, and sister in this work. Your support and friendship mean everything to me, and I am beyond grateful for the countless ways you have pushed me to keep going.

To my big sisters and mother, Minnie Springfield—you were my first example of resilience and perseverance in a world that did not always make space for Black girls. Watching you navigate spaces that were not always welcoming, yet refusing to shrink, gave me the courage to do the same. Mama, you were my first teacher. The way you poured into your students with love, patience, and unwavering dedication showed me what it truly means to be an educator. You modeled passion, excellence, and care, leaving an indelible mark on me. Thank you all for paving the way, inspiring me, and showing me how to lead—with knowledge and heart. And thank you, Daddy, Odell Springfield, for always seeing the little girl in me, even if the world refused to.

While I have named a few, I have certainly been influenced by many. I wish I could list every name of every person who has offered encouragement, a smile, a hug, or a high five, but those thank-yous would be the length of another book. Please know that I carry your support with me and am grateful beyond measure.

To the Black girls I have had the honor of teaching, mentoring, and advocating for—thank you for inspiring me, daily, with your brilliance, resilience, laughter, creativity, passion, and courage.

Jericho, my love, my partner, my greatest supporter—thank you for holding me up, believing in me when I doubted myself, and reminding me why this work matters. Your love and encouragement have kept me grounded, and I am endlessly grateful for you.

Madison and Miah, my sweet, brilliant daughters—you are my greatest inspiration. Every word of this book is written with you in mind. You are powerful beyond measure, your voices matter, and you never have to dim your light for anyone. You are the reason I fight, the reason I push forward, and the reason I refuse to settle for a world that does not fully embrace the beauty and brilliance of Black girls.

This book is more than words on a page—it is a love letter, a call to action, and a declaration that Black girls deserve to be seen, heard, protected, and celebrated.

About the Author

Dr. Melody Hawkins is an award-winning educator, author, and visionary leader dedicated to transforming education for students in historically underserved communities. A passionate advocate for equity in urban education, Melody has spent her career ensuring that all students—particularly those from ethnically and culturally diverse backgrounds—have access to inclusive, high-quality learning experiences that prepare them for lifelong success.

A former eighth-grade science teacher, Melody infused her instruction with culturally relevant pedagogy and social-emotional learning, inspiring students to see themselves as scientists, innovators, and changemakers. She later transitioned into educational leadership as a high school administrator, where she continues to champion equitable opportunities for students while mentoring educators in fostering meaningful, identity-affirming learning environments. In addition to her school work, Melody collaborates with community-based organizations, helping them maximize the impact of their programs and initiatives to better serve and empower the youth in their communities.

Melody's journey in education began after earning a bachelor's degree in microbiology from the University of Tennessee. Her commitment to service led her to AmeriCorps, where she worked with the American Red Cross in New Orleans, Louisiana. After a successful career in diagnostic laboratory science, she recognized the urgent need for more representation of scientists of color and pivoted to education—channeling her expertise into science instruction. She earned a master of education in curriculum and instruction, followed by a second master's degree in educational leadership, through a Tennessee Department of Education administrator development program.

She completed her doctorate in organizational innovation at National University.

A nationally recognized leader in education, Melody has served on state- and district-level curriculum teams, assessment committees, and educator fellowships. Her outstanding contributions have earned her numerous accolades, including Knox County Schools Middle School Science Teacher of the Year, and recognition as one of Knoxville's 40 Under 40 Most Influential People. In a moment of national recognition, she was surprised with the 2021 National University Teacher of the Year Award on the *Drew Barrymore Show*, a testament to her impact and dedication as an educator. She has also been honored by the Tennessee General Assembly and the City of Jackson, Tennessee, for her work in education.

Beyond her professional accomplishments, Melody is a devoted wife to Jericho, a fellow University of Tennessee alum, and a proud mother to their two daughters, Madison and Miah. She resides in Tennessee, where she continues to inspire educators, empower students, and support organizations committed to creating lasting, positive change for youth.

Navigating *Black Girl in the Middle*

DEFINING "BLACK GIRL"

For the purposes of this book, "Black girl" refers to individuals who self-identify as girls and align with the cultural and racial identities tied to the African diaspora. This encompasses a wide spectrum of experiences, skin tones, languages, and cultural traditions. It includes girls with ancestry rooted in Africa, whether they are African American, Afro-Caribbean, African immigrants, or part of multiracial communities who identify with their Black heritage.

It is important to recognize that Black girlhood is not monolithic. While shared experiences of navigating systemic inequities may unite many Black girls, their identities are shaped by a rich diversity of histories, geographies, and family traditions. This book is grounded in honoring this complexity while affirming the shared need for support, representation, and understanding in educational spaces.

IS THIS JUST FOR WHITE EDUCATORS?

Absolutely not. *Black Girl in the Middle* is for all educators, mentors, and supporters of Black girls—regardless of their racial or cultural background. While it is true that white educators may need to confront biases or blind spots when working with Black girls, this book goes beyond merely addressing those gaps. As a Black woman, I have learned so much through the research and findings presented here—concepts and perspectives I had never deeply considered before engaging with this work.

This book is a journey of discovery and reflection for anyone who interacts with Black girls, including Black educators like myself. It challenges us all to see how systemic inequities, implicit biases, and unexamined practices influence our work. By acknowledging these dynamics and leaning into culturally responsive and affirming practices, we can all do better in uplifting the brilliance, creativity, and resilience of Black girls.

WHO SHOULD READ
BLACK GIRL IN THE MIDDLE?

This book is for anyone who is committed to creating affirming, inclusive, and equitable spaces for Black girls in middle school. Whether you're a teacher, school administrator, mentor, counselor, parent, or community leader, *Black Girl in the Middle* offers valuable insights and strategies to support Black girls in navigating educational spaces that often fail to fully see and celebrate them.

It's particularly essential for educators and leaders who want to do more than just acknowledge systemic inequities—they want to actively dismantle them. This book is also for those who may already be doing the work but want to deepen their understanding of the unique challenges and strengths of Black girls.

Ultimately, this book is for anyone who believes in the power of education to affirm, empower, and inspire every student to thrive, particularly those who are most often overlooked or misunderstood.

UNDERSTANDING KEY
TERMS AND CONCEPTS

The key terms and concepts listed here are interconnected and reinforce a system where racial and gender biases are perpetuated in subtle but powerful ways, influencing the way students of color, especially Black students, experience education. By understanding and addressing these ideas, educators can begin to break down barriers to equity and create more inclusive, culturally responsive learning environments.

> **Data sources** refer to the various ways in which information is collected and analyzed to understand the experiences of students within the education system. These sources can include standardized test scores, attendance records, behavioral referrals, teacher evaluations, surveys, and qualitative data from student interviews and focus groups. However, when data collection fails to consider systemic biases—such as the impact of race, gender, and adultification bias—the resulting insights can perpetuate inequities rather than address them.[1] For Black girls, understanding which data sources are being used and how they are interpreted is crucial for uncovering hidden disparities in discipline, academic performance, and social-emotional supports.

Race and ethnicity are social constructs used to classify individuals based on perceived physical characteristics (race) and cultural factors such as language, ancestry, and traditions (ethnicity). For Black girls, their racial and ethnic identities play a significant role in shaping their experiences in predominantly white educational spaces, often leading to stereotyping, implicit bias, and systemic inequities. Black girls are frequently perceived through deficit lenses, which ignore their resilience, brilliance, and cultural richness.[2] Acknowledging and affirming the intersection of race and ethnicity is essential for creating spaces where Black girls can thrive academically, socially, and emotionally.

Gender refers to the socially constructed roles, behaviors, and expectations associated with being male, female, or nonbinary. For Black girls, the intersection of their gender and race results in unique challenges that are often overlooked in schools. Misconceptions about Black girls, such as assumptions about their behavior, emotionality, or academic abilities, are rooted in historical stereotypes that continue to shape how they are perceived and treated in the classroom.[3] Understanding the intersectionality of gender and race allows educators to see Black girls as multidimensional individuals who deserve respect, encouragement, and equitable opportunities to succeed.

Adultification bias refers to the tendency to perceive Black girls as older, more mature, and less innocent than their white peers of the same age. This bias often leads to harsher discipline, reduced empathy from adults, and higher expectations for behavior that fail to consider the developmental needs of children.[4] For example, Black girls are disproportionately punished for behaviors that might be seen as playful or age-appropriate in other students. Recognizing and countering adultification bias is critical for ensuring that Black girls receive the care, guidance, and grace they need to grow into their full potential.

Microaggressions are subtle, often unintentional, verbal or behavioral slights that communicate discriminatory or prejudiced messages, particularly against marginalized groups. In the classroom, microaggressions can take the form of seemingly innocent comments or actions that reinforce stereotypes, such as assuming a student's intelligence based on their race or making generalized statements about cultural behaviors. These small but impactful moments accumulate over time, leading to negative consequences for students' sense of belonging and self-worth.

Cultural assimilation refers to the process by which students are expected to abandon or suppress their cultural identities in favor of adopting mainstream (often white) cultural norms and practices. In schools, this can be reflected in behaviors, such as expecting students to conform to Eurocentric ideas of appropriate behavior, communication, and even modes of learning. This practice overlooks the richness and validity of diverse cultural backgrounds, creating environments where students must "fit in" at the expense of their authentic selves.

Colorblindness in education refers to the practice of ignoring or downplaying the significance of race and ethnicity in the classroom. When educators claim to be "colorblind," they may believe they are treating all students equally, but in reality, they may be overlooking the unique experiences and needs of students from different racial or ethnic backgrounds. This approach can prevent educators from acknowledging the impact of systemic racism and inequality, making it harder to address the specific challenges faced by students of color.

Ethnic-racial identity refers to the way individuals understand and define themselves in relation to their ethnic and racial backgrounds. This process of identity formation is influenced by both internal factors (such as personal experiences and beliefs) and external factors (such as societal attitudes and biases). For Black girls, the intersection of race and gender can create a unique and often challenging path in developing their identity in a society that holds conflicting expectations about who they should be.

The belief gap refers to the phenomenon in which some educators lack belief in the potential of students from low-income backgrounds and students of color, often driven by negative stereotypes that go unchallenged within schools. This lack of belief can contribute to systemic inequities and perpetuate low expectations, limiting opportunities and outcomes for these students. This can show up in a variety of ways, including lowering academic standards for students of color, offering less assistance and support, and not pushing them as hard in the classroom. The belief gap also extends to society at large, where there is often a reluctance to invest in educational resources and teachers for these students.

The deficit mindset focuses on what students lack or the problems they face. It tends to highlight weaknesses, gaps in skills, and deficits in students' knowledge or behavior, often viewing students in a one-dimensional way. This perspective emphasizes what students cannot do rather than what they can do, leading to low expectations. In a classroom with a deficit mindset, a teacher might view a student struggling with reading as "lazy" or "not capable," focusing only on remedial interventions to "fix" the student. This approach risks reinforcing stereotypes or biases, especially for students from marginalized backgrounds, and can limit opportunities for growth.

The strengths-based mindset emphasizes students' existing strengths, abilities, and potential. It focuses on what students can do and how these strengths can be leveraged to overcome challenges. This perspective promotes a more holistic view of students, recognizing that everyone has unique qualities and capacities for growth. A teacher using a strengths-based approach might identify a student's creativity or problem-solving skills, building assignments that allow the student to apply these strengths while also improving their reading. This mindset fosters a positive, growth-oriented environment, increases student engagement, and empowers students to take ownership of their learning.

Culturally responsive teaching, not to be confused with critical race theory, is a well-researched and evolving field that focuses on integrating students' cultural backgrounds into teaching practices to create more inclusive, equitable, and empowering learning environments. Culturally responsive teaching emphasizes recognizing and valuing the diverse identities and experiences that students bring to the classroom, adapting curricula, teaching methods, and assessments to reflect and affirm these identities while promoting academic success and social justice.

Here is a list of some foundational books and research studies that have significantly contributed to the development and understanding of culturally responsive teaching:

Aronson, B., & Laughter, J. (2016). The theory and practice of culturally relevant education: A synthesis of research across content areas. *Review of Educational Research, 86*(1).

Gay, G. (2000).*Culturally responsive teaching: Theory, research, and practice.* Teachers College Press.

Gay, G. (2002). Preparing for culturally responsive teaching. *Journal of Teacher Education, 53*(2).

Hammond, Z. (2014). *Culturally responsive teaching and the brain: Promoting authentic engagement and rigor among culturally and linguistically diverse students.* Corwin.

Ladson-Billings, G. (1995). Toward a theory of culturally relevant pedagogy. *American Educational Research Journal, 32*(3).

Paris, D. (2012). Culturally sustaining pedagogy: A needed change in stance, terminology, and practice. *Educational Researcher, 41*(3).

Paris, D. (2021). Culturally sustaining pedagogies and our futures. *The Educational Forum, 85*(4), 364–376.

Paris, D., & Alim, S. H. (2014). What are we seeking to sustain through culturally sustaining pedagogy? A loving critique forward. *Harvard Educational Review, 84*(1).

Coverage of race, opportunity, and equity is supported in part by a grant from The Wallace Foundation, at www.wallacefoundation.org. Education Week retains sole editorial control over the content of this coverage.

A version of this article appeared in the May 11, 2022, edition of *Education Week* titled "What Is Culturally Responsive Teaching?"

NOTES

1. Muhammad, G. (2020). *Cultivating genius: An equity framework for culturally and historically responsive literacy.* Scholastic.

2. Collins, P. H. (2000). *Black feminist thought: Knowledge, consciousness, and the politics of empowerment.* Routledge.

3. Murray, P. (2017). *Girlhood interrupted: The erasure of Black girls' childhood.* The Georgetown Law Center on Poverty and Inequality. Retrieved July 1, 2022, from https://genderjusticeandopportunity.georgetown.edu/wp-content/uploads/2020/06/girlhood-interrupted.pdf

4. Murray (2017).

Introduction

WHY IS SHE SITTING ALONE?

I was in preschool the first time I realized I was being treated differently from other kids around me. Preschool—which would mean I was approaching five years old. My earliest memory of preschool involves being dropped at a building that felt dark and lonely, despite it likely being adorned with the abstract artwork of toddlers discovering the expressions of art, letter making, and number recognition.

I do not remember the colors, the crafts, or the classroom displays, but I remember how I felt. I felt scared. I felt different. The kind of difference that made me feel as if I did not belong. I was shy and quiet and wanted to play with other kids, but I never felt like they wanted to play with me. I vividly remember my mother picking me up from school one day and asking the teacher why I was always sitting alone. I do not remember the teacher's answer, but my mother's response is clear: "Please gather Melody's things. We will not be returning after today."

My mother, a teacher, has always had a way of making people feel her words. She is small, but her words can make any giant feel tiny. Whatever the teacher said, my mother did not find it an acceptable answer. I can narrowly recall that day as a four-year-old, having placed that memory away into a special corner of my brain. The memory resurfaced when I had my first daughter, Madison. My husband, Jericho, and I were beginning the search for a preschool for her, and, like many parents, we wanted to ensure she would be in a safe and loving space. I also felt intensely passionate about Madison being in a space that honored her as a little Black girl. This meant a space where she would never feel isolated or out of place, even if she was the only Black girl in the room.

As my own experiences began to shine through the deepest parts of my memory, I wanted to make sure Madison never felt alone and that she could show up as her beautiful brown self with beads and braids. Recalling what the four-year-old version of me remembered, I asked my mother more about that day at "that" preschool. Although a distant memory for both of us, she could still remember clearly what the teacher said to her when my mother asked, "Why is Melody always sitting alone?" The teacher's response was "Because she wants to. She never wants to play with the other kids." As an educator, my mother quickly realized the problem with this statement. The problem reveals a lack of concern for a child's social and emotional development. Although preschool is most widely known for developing academic agility and social skills, it was not a priority to this preschool teacher, seeing that there was no urgency to encourage this little girl (me) to interact with her peers.

Whenever I have shared this story with my colleagues or friends, they always ask, "Were you the only Black girl in the preschool?" And, yes, yes, I was. In fact, I was the only Black person in the building. It is a critical point within the context of this memory. Maybe my preschool teacher thought I was "okay," not playing with others. She may have even thought that it was okay for me to make my own choices and that I was *choosing* to be alone daily, with little to no interaction with other students my age. Or is it possible that the preschool teacher simply did not feel that I needed the same interactions and nurturing as other students, which is the thinking that is consistent with a historic construct about Black girls?

These were all of my thoughts as my husband and I were choosing a place for Madison to begin her learning journey. It might be difficult to imagine an adult would think a child needs less nurturing, less care, and less social development, but this is precisely the thinking about Black girls. Research studies show that Black girls are regularly treated as if they are adults. A 2017 study titled *Girlhood Interrupted* by Georgetown Law's Center on Poverty and Inequality shows that adults tend to view Black girls between the ages of 5 and 19 as more adult than their white counterparts.[1] The study also found that adults viewed five-year-old Black girls as behaving older than their age, more aware of adult topics, and more likely to take on adult responsibilities than expected for their age. As the only Black person and the only Black female student, I was likely exposed to some of these thoughts. These thoughts would directly influence how I was treated in my preschool environment and impact my sense of belonging among the other students. Remember me stating that I felt like I was being treated differently? Even as a young child, I could feel it.

My mother swiftly moved me to a well-known community preschool in east Jackson, Tennessee. In this place, I was not the only Black girl; I was not the only Black person. My teachers were all Black women. They were firm but affirming. I was able to flourish and fly to kindergarten thanks to their support. Now, even beyond the obvious point of not being the only Black girl in the preschool class, what made my new preschool different from my previous preschool was how the adults connected with me as a little Black girl. I never felt alone or isolated. My days were filled with freedom, fun, structure, expectations, and belonging. I felt like I belonged. Perhaps the adults knew how to create this space for me because they were Black women. Yes, this point is true. But what about the next Black girl who would attend my previous preschool? Does she not also deserve to feel like she belongs? The feeling of "belonging" can do wonders for a young student's academic and social-emotional development as it is positively associated with success. It is not simply a nice-to-have; it is a foundational element for young students' success. Research demonstrates that when students feel a strong sense of belonging in school, they are more likely to engage in learning, build resilience, and perform better academically.[2] This connection fosters intrinsic motivation and supports healthy self-concept development, which are critical for both academic achievement and social-emotional well-being.[3]

Moreover, belonging enhances students' ability to form meaningful relationships and navigate challenges, leading to increased motivation and a deeper commitment to learning.[4] For Black girls, who may face unique challenges in predominantly white educational spaces, intentional efforts by educators to create inclusive environments can close equity gaps and ensure they feel valued and supported.[5]

This means it is critically important that all adults who work with Black girls in an educational setting recognize how important it is to create belonging for young Black girls.

Despite my preschool experience as a young student, I can remember having an optimistic view of my educational future. My mother, currently a retired educator, kept me inspired and focused on a successful journey through education. I was an overachieving honor student who always sought ways to deepen my understanding and learn more. Although I had a positive mindset about my education, I did not always have positive experiences in school.

As a Black girl in elementary school, I was often among the few students of color in my honors classes. By the time I reached middle school age, I noticed a systemic separation among my peers. Students of lower socioeconomic status and students of color were less represented in conversations about high academic achievement and advanced academic classes. I knew then that this was not acceptable. However, I was unsure if anyone else noticed or even cared. As I progressed through my college journey, the representation of students from low socio-economic levels was not as noticeable. The lack of Black persons represented in higher education was still a recognizable problem. By this time, I knew that the leaders in charge of supporting schools were paying attention to this lack of representation, but I could not help feeling uneasy about how they were going about fixing it. Some of the efforts seemed to only scratch the surface, as if they were just checking boxes instead of digging deeper to figure out the real problem. For example, there were programs to bring in more diverse faces, but no one seemed to be asking, "What happens after that?" Were these individuals being set up to thrive, or were they just being added to a system that was not designed with them in mind?

It also felt like these ideas were not being carried out consistently, so whatever progress was made seemed patchy at best. And in some cases, the plans themselves felt flawed—plans such as offering training that focused on cultural awareness but stopped short of showing people how to use those lessons to make classrooms or leadership spaces more inclusive. To me, it was not just about fixing numbers; it was about creating spaces where people from marginalized groups felt like they belonged and could succeed. At that point, I was not seeing enough of that.

From as far back as 1799, when John Chavis, a Presbyterian minister and teacher, was the first Black person on record to attend an American college or university, Black persons' access to higher education had been an elephant in any room about postsecondary attainments.[6] After nearly 200 years of occasional individual cases of Black individuals being granted access to higher education institutions, U.S. colleges and universities finally began moving to more pointed efforts to ensure equitable access to higher education. Following a 1992 Supreme Court ruling in *United States v. Fordice* that ordered 19 states to take immediate action to desegregate their public higher education systems, various initiatives were implemented to boost Black student enrollment in the United States, especially at state-funded universities and predominantly white institutions (PWIs). These initiatives included outreach programs targeting high schools with significant Black populations, scholarship opportunities specifically for Black students, race-sensitive considerations in admissions policies, and establishing cultural centers or affinity groups on campuses, such as Minority Enhancement for the University of Tennessee, an initiative formed to promote the diversity advantage of the University of Tennessee.[7] While these efforts initially led to an increase in enrollment, they often fell short in retaining Black students due to a lack of understanding of the importance of inclusion, anti-bias practices, and cultural belonging. As a Black college student at a PWI, I experienced and witnessed Black students face challenges such as feelings of isolation, lack of support networks, and encounters with racial discrimination on campus, which distracted us from academic success and sometimes led to higher dropout rates. What I quickly realized while a college student was that institutions that do not address the systemic barriers that Black students face once enrolled are likely to perpetuate inequity and limit success. Without adequate support systems and a sense of belonging, many Black students struggled to persist and graduate from college. These truths impacted me and fueled my desire to stay focused on dismantling these barriers for the next generation of Black students.

When I decided to become an educator in an urban setting, I knew I wanted to do my part to increase Black student representation in higher education. I also aimed to ensure that I supported all students from low socioeconomic environments in achieving postsecondary success, whether in college or a career. Without surprise, I am passionate about the academic growth and achievement of Black students, particularly those students who live in historically underserved communities in the United States.

As an educator in an urban setting, I have witnessed most students experience disparities in access to this high-quality education. Because of this, I have had to teach with a great purpose and vision, birthed from my belief in the students I serve. My vision is that I will provide daily instruction that allows students to identify their strengths as learners, collaborate, and solve problems so that students, particularly Black students, will receive access to high-quality, equitable education that allows them to make positive contributions to their community. I developed this vision at the end of my first year in the classroom. That is why I show up every day for my students. My vision is what keeps me persistently providing my students with high-quality instruction. Every opportunity to speak to my students is anchored with this vision. Academic conversations are infused with social-emotional skills, and everyday life conversations are infused with academic content. My vision has become the foundation of who I am as an educator.

I am always peeling back the layers of what this vision means and how it looks in practice and action. With each new school year also comes the need to reexamine my students' experiences in school and their experiences in the greater community. I must become familiar with my students' perspectives to fully commit to working toward my vision. Of all the different perspectives our students bring to the classroom, the perspective of a Black girl in academic settings has always stood out to me. As an educator, I continue to see inequities in the treatment of Black girls in education, and as a Black woman, I have experienced these firsthand. I do not teach or lead from a place of lack. So often, while I am in the zone of teaching, instructing, facilitating, supporting, and working with my students to build their academic and social-emotional character, I do not think about what I lacked as a student. I instead focus on what I know my students need at that very moment. And that is where knowing their perspectives comes into practice. My students may approach a challenging task partly because of what they have previously experienced regarding challenges. The way my students may approach a challenging task, which might include trepidation or doubt, is influenced by their past experiences. This suggests that prior encounters with similar challenges, whether successful or not, shape their confidence levels and strategies for tackling new obstacles. For instance, a student who struggled with math in elementary school may approach a complex algebra problem with hesitation, drawing upon memories of previous difficulties, while another student who excelled in science competitions may tackle the same problem with greater confidence, buoyed by past successes. By recognizing the unique experiences and challenges Black girls face in academic settings, I can create a classroom environment that supports their individual needs and fosters their growth and success.

The importance of understanding a student's perspective hit me when a student abruptly interrupted my lesson on the Galaxy movement. She stated, "Ms. Hawkins, I can't believe you're my teacher." I was standing at the whiteboard illustrating the evidence connected to the movement of galaxies in our universe, but her statement stopped my hand from moving. With awe and passion, she continued, "Like, you're a Black woman teaching me science. And you know what you're talking about. That's so cool. I usually see white people talking about science." I paused, looked at my beautiful Black student with the same awe she gave me, and told her, "That's right. And you are a Black girl who understands what I'm talking about. That's even cooler." I left the building that day and have never let that moment slip from my memory. She was an eighth-grade girl experiencing an empowering moment in her academic journey simply by seeing herself reflected in her Black woman science teacher.

I could be wrong in assuming that she had not seen herself reflected in her previous teachers, but the staggeringly low percentage of Black teachers in the United States would say that she likely had not. Although research supports the positive impact of Black educators on student achievement and social-emotional growth, with only 7% of the teacher workforce in the United States identifying as a Black educator, perhaps this is one reason racial disparities in academic achievement continue to exist.[8] Not only do Black educators increase the probability of achievement for Black students, but Black educators also allow all students to experience racial and cultural diversity in preparation for a diverse world. Black students want and need to see Black educators in their classrooms. All students can benefit from being taught by a Black educator as this prepares them for a diverse workforce. In a thought-provoking article by the American Economic Association in 2023, a professor and authority in education and labor economics, Seth Gershenson, shared an insightful perspective.[9] He stated, "White students benefit as well from being exposed to a diverse and representative teaching force; . . . having a teacher of color can shift their worldview and sense of who can do what. It can shape their racial attitudes in a beneficial and prosocial way." Gershenson's words underscore the profound influence that a diverse teaching faculty, particularly Black educators, can have on shaping not only students' academic experiences but also their broader outlook and attitudes toward race.

In my heart, I always felt that having a Black educator was a treasure, and as a scientist, I have spent the last 10 years reading the data that support this. Data such as higher graduation rates for Black students, increased achievement scores, lower suspension rates, and higher interest in college have all been linked to a Black teacher's presence as the classroom teacher. A 2019 Brookings Institution article by Andre Perry highlights the positive impact of having Black teachers in the classroom, emphasizing several key points. First, it suggests that Black students who have had at least one Black teacher are more likely to graduate high school and aspire to attend college.[10] Additionally, exposure to Black teachers correlates with higher college attendance rates among Black students. Furthermore, the presence of Black teachers has been linked to reduced dropout rates for Black students and increased likelihood of pursuing postsecondary education.

Black educators make a difference by showing up as our authentic selves. I am a Black woman, full of pride, with a love for science and a passion for seeing young people become their best selves. I am also a demanding nurturer, striving not only to challenge my students academically but also to cultivate an environment where they feel valued, supported, and empowered to reach their full potential. While drawing inspiration from Rita Pierson's concept of the warm demander, I extend this notion further by emphasizing the importance of nurturing students' emotional well-being, fostering their personal growth, and instilling in them a deep sense of self-confidence and resilience. As a warm demander, I believe in fostering not just academic excellence but also the holistic development of each student, recognizing that their success extends beyond the classroom and into their lives. I show up as all of those things without apology. I know that my students are watching my every move, and I take responsibility with the utmost importance to demonstrate a character they can draw from in pursuit of who they are in this world. Now, as we drift back to my awe-stricken student, consider her perspective while watching her Black female science teacher—a mirror of her future, perhaps—a mirror that she might never have seen in her classroom before.

In addition to the likely low chance that my student had more Black teachers other than me, I can even take a wild guess and assume that she may not have experienced positive, safe spaces cultivated with Black girls in mind during her time in school.

My firsthand knowledge as a Black girl in an academic setting can support this theory. However, to truly grasp the extent of these issues, we must turn to the groundbreaking research project "Listening to Black Women and Girls: Lived Experiences of Adultification Bias."[11] This study serves as a continuation of the *Girlhood Interrupted* report released by the Georgetown Law Center on Poverty and Inequality in 2017. The project illuminates the pervasive nature of Black women and girls' treatment in our society through rigorous qualitative methods like interviews and focus groups. This experience may not be as obvious without peeling back the undertones of statements commonly made.

The findings from this report, accompanied by the poignant voices of Black women and girls, paint a stark picture of the injustices they face. Participants across various age groups share their experiences, highlighting the denial of their childhood innocence and the imposition of premature expectations. As one participant in the 30- to 39-year age group poignantly expresses, "[T]here's, like, this non-acceptance of being a child."[12] Younger participants echo this sentiment, describing how they are held to adult-like standards from a young age, facing severe consequences for ordinary childhood mistakes.

Moreover, the study reveals how deeply ingrained stereotypes like the "angry Black woman" narrative shape perceptions and interactions. Participants recount instances of being labeled as insubordinate or having attitude problems simply for expressing themselves. This unfair treatment extends to disciplinary actions, often resulting in punitive measures rather than support and guidance.

The hyper-sexualization of Black girls is also a prevalent theme in their narratives. The study recounts instances where their clothing choices are misconstrued, and their innocence is questioned. Additionally, societal expectations of white norm femininity stifle their voices and invalidate their experiences. As one participant aptly says, "They just wanna shut us off. They just want us to be—be quiet . . . whenever we start to talk, nothing's happening."

These reflections shed light on the intersectional nature of adultification bias, which is compounded by factors such as race, age, socioeconomic status, and gender. As another participant poignantly notes, "Black girls in poor families do have to grow up. It's about socioeconomics, too. It's not just about . . . being Black." And, as if it was my voice captured in this report, a participant from the 18- to 29-year age group stated, "At the preschool point is where teachers are starting to feel like . . . 'Black girls are a little too sassy.'" These insights appear in multiple societal locations, particularly in the criminal legal system and education. In the education system, adultification bias against Black girls leads to less opportunity for Black girls to be in class learning with their peers and, therefore, lower academic achievement rates. There is clearly an urgent need for systemic change to dismantle the structures that perpetuate negative experiences and ensure that Black women and girls are afforded the dignity, respect, and opportunities they rightfully deserve.

After my student's statement, I drove home thinking more about my vision for my students and why I teach. My aim is to provide academic experiences where my students can learn to become positive contributors to the community. To provide experiences for our students to grow and thrive, we must understand our students' perspectives. My student's perspective was that she had disproportionately learned science content from white teachers. Her perspective lacked the presence of racial representation that was similar to her own. Due to the implicit biases of her teachers, her perspective potentially lacked opportunities to feel a sense of belonging in her academic spaces. These are things I had to understand about my student's academic experiences. I can still recall when a Black woman, a mentor, told me I would have "two strikes against me." I was a sixth-grade middle school student. The two strikes she referred to were my race and my gender. At the intersection of racism and sexism, there stands a Black girl.

Why shouldn't we explore how to create supportive spaces in academic settings for Black girls? If we truly believe that all students deserve fair and appropriate public education, we must consider how Black girls are forced to exist in the middle of racism and sexism and how this shows up in their schools and classrooms.

WHY FOCUS ON MIDDLE SCHOOL YEARS?

When I first received the vision for *Black Girl in the Middle*, it immediately felt like more than a book. It began to take on a form in my mind that resembled a pedagogical movement for middle school educators. As an educator who has worked with students between the ages of 10 and 18, as a mom of my own two Black girls, and as a Black woman, I have noticed that the middle school years, typically between ages 10 and 14, are very critical in the academic, social, and emotional success of Black girls.

These years are a formative period when identity, self-esteem, and academic confidence take shape, and it's also when young Black girls begin to grapple more deeply with what it means to be Black—and specifically, a Black girl—in the United States. Research supports how pivotal this age range is: adolescence marks a period of heightened vulnerability to social pressures and stereotypes that can significantly impact both academic motivation and self-perception.[13] I have seen this with my adolescent girls and can vividly remember these feelings as an adolescent. At the same time, supportive environments that emphasize positive racial and gender identity can foster resilience and a stronger sense of self-worth.[14]

The pressure Black girls face is unique; during these years, they are often perceived as more mature than their peers—a phenomenon known as "adultification"—which can lead to higher disciplinary rates, diminished emotional support, and fewer chances to fully experience childhood.[15] Such experiences, left unaddressed, can hinder their academic engagement and social-emotional development. Yet, with intentional guidance, these years hold the potential to shape Black girls into empowered young women who see their identities as strengths rather than limitations.

Black Girl in the Middle seeks to be part of that journey, helping to create environments where Black girls feel seen, heard, and celebrated in the ways they need most during these critical middle school years.

My goal in writing this book is not to simplify the experiences of Black girls into a monolithic category, nor is it intended to single out the experiences of Black girls in school as the only group with a harsher experience. Instead, I write this book to ensure that all persons privileged with the opportunity to support Black girls in their academic journey will have strategies for creating an inclusive, nurturing, supportive environment where our girls can experience limitless success. I also hope that educators will have a deepened perspective about the circumstances Black girls are faced with, in hopes that educators will work to transform these experiences. The reality is that public education, at its first inception, was not created with Black girls in mind. The reality is harsh but true. But "we are here, and we are not leaving," says the Black girl in me. So instead of trying to fit the unlimited potential of Black girls into a square that was not designed for them, perhaps it is time that we remove the boundaries of the square (and here "the square" refers to the historic and, at times, antiquated structure of public education) and focus on creating an experience that our Black girls can feel more comfortable in and thrive.

FIVE PRACTICES FOR ENHANCING LEARNING FOR BLACK GIRLS

The five practices that I have detailed in this book are based on my experiences of teaching young Black girls, the efforts of my colleagues, and the research that exists in support of improving academic spaces for Black girls. When I reflect on my opportunities to support my Black girl students, these practices are the ones that I can vividly remember making a positive impact on the interaction and thus catapulting my students toward more confidence and greater success. These are the practices that I have witnessed my colleagues implement with an unyielding effort. These are the practices that—as you'll see in future chapters—research sustains with documented influence. I introduce these practices now as questions and will explain them in greater detail in the coming chapters. Allow the questions to ring in your mind. Think back on every encounter you have had with your Black girl students. Return to a moment when you were delivering a lesson, walking down the hallway, passing through the cafeteria, approaching the tutoring table, or standing at your morning or afternoon spot as the hallways, doorways, and sidewalks filled with students. See the faces of the Black girls as I ask these questions:

- **Practice 1—Identify Your Beliefs:** What do you believe about the social-emotional and academic presence of Black girls? How do your actions communicate this belief?

- **Practice 2—Plant the SEAD:** How do you support the social-emotional and academic growth of Black girls? Are your actions *intentional* in fostering both their emotional well-being and academic success?

- **Practice 3—Listen With Compassion:** How do you demonstrate compassionate listening? Are you listening to what they say, how they say, and what they really are communicating to you?

- **Practice 4—Encourage Positive Self-Talk:** When and how do you encourage positive self-talk? Are you intentional about encouraging self-affirming thoughts and fostering their sense of worth?

- **Practice 5—Advocate for Their Girlhood:** How do you respond to Black girls academically and socially? Do you engage with Black girls in age-appropriate ways, honoring their developmental stage and individuality?

Maybe you think of questions like these regarding all of your students. That's great. But guess what's more remarkable—pausing and thinking of these questions specifically for Black girls who may not have had these questions considered within the context of their educational existence in the United States. If there is any uncertainty about your answers to any of these questions as they pertain to Black girl students, then now is the moment to reflect and identify how these are embedded in your everyday interactions. It is a great moment to point out that these are "practices," not "steps," meaning that any thoughts can be implemented at any time but must be consistently implemented. Although these practices are not prescriptive, nor intended to be a "take a pill; make it better" kind of mindset, they must become a way of life in the classroom, intentionally focused on Black girls. If done frequently, I believe these practices will change the experience for our Black girls and certainly positively impact all Black students and students of color. That would be a well-deserved outcome for students of color. Suffice it to say, it is past the time that we focus on the student group forced to thrive in the middle of racism and sexism, our Black girls.

USING THIS BOOK

GUIDING THE JOURNEY TO REFLECT, BUILD, AND ADVOCATE

The division of this book into *Reflect*, *Build*, and *Advocate* mirrors the journey that every educator is invited to take—a journey that begins with introspection, moves through purposeful action, and culminates in meaningful advocacy. Just as I was able to sense, even as a young child, the subtle shifts and quiet signals that told me I was being treated differently, Black girls sense and interpret the attitudes, actions, and support (or lack thereof) they receive from the adults around them. They navigate classrooms and learning spaces that can feel dark and isolating or, with intention, vibrant and empowering. This division of the book is a response to that reality, providing a pathway for educators to recognize, understand, and dismantle the barriers that may prevent Black girls from feeling fully welcomed in academic spaces.

Each section goes beyond simply offering information; it equips you with practical strategies and actionable steps. **Part 1: *Reflect* on Beliefs and Biases** encourages you to examine your own beliefs and biases, challenging you to look inward, but it also provides tools for confronting and reshaping those beliefs to better serve your students. Chapter 1, "It's Not My Fault; It Is My Problem," tackles the deep-rooted issues Black girls face in the education system and the historical context that has shaped these challenges. Here, you'll be encouraged to take ownership of the impact you have and to recognize how your beliefs shape students' lives. Chapter 2, "Practice One—Identify Your Beliefs" explores stereotypes and invites you to examine any unconscious biases you may hold. Here, you'll find tools to confront and dismantle stereotypes, learning to value each student's unique strengths and identities.

In **Part 2: Build Compassionate and Supportive Connections**, the focus shifts to creating a foundation of trust and empathy. You'll not only be guided to form compassionate, genuine connections, but you'll also receive hands-on approaches for creating a classroom that feels safe, inclusive, and affirming. Chapter 3, "Practice Two—Plant the SEAD," presents strategies for fostering an inclusive classroom, with specific approaches for addressing social-emotional-academic development. The goal here is to make sure each student feels they belong in a safe and supportive learning environment. Moving forward, Chapter 4, "Practice Three—Listen With Compassion," teaches you the art of compassionate listening, guiding you in understanding Black girls as whole individuals. This chapter includes exercises that foster genuine empathy, encouraging you to take a deeper interest in each student's background, challenges, and dreams.

In **Part 3:** *Advocate* **for Her Development and Childhood,** you'll learn how to empower and advocate for Black girls. You're given ways to put this deeper understanding into action—actively championing the unique needs and rights of Black girls, preserving their girlhood, fostering their self-assurance, and ensuring they feel seen and valued. Chapter 5, "Practice Four—Encourage Positive Self-Talk," focuses on building confidence, self-advocacy, and leadership skills, helping each girl learn to express herself with conviction. This chapter provides practical ways to nurture self-worth, allowing students to see themselves as capable leaders. Chapter 6, "Practice Five—Advocate for Their Girlhood," addresses the adultification of Black girls and the pressure to "know better." You'll find insights into respecting and preserving their girlhood, encouraging you to create a classroom that honors their journey. Chapter 7, "Partnering With Families and Communities," expands the conversation to include families and community figures, teaching you how to cultivate a broad support network through culturally relevant engagement and mentorship.

Finally, in the Conclusion, "Transforming Learning for Black Girls," you'll reflect on the journey, revisit key themes, and learn how to embed these practices into school culture as lasting change. The closing chapter offers tools for ongoing assessment, encouraging you to implement and revisit these practices to sustain a supportive environment for Black girls.

At the end of each chapter, you'll find a reflection section titled **"In the Middle."** This is more than a title—it signifies a commitment to centering Black girls' experiences. **"In the Middle"** invites you to examine your practices, challenge biases, and focus on the voices and needs of Black girls. Through this process, you'll engage deeply with the historical and present-day realities shaping their educational journeys and take intentional steps toward creating environments where they can thrive.

Let each reflection be a moment of **reckoning, learning,** *and* **taking action** as you navigate this journey. Stay "in the middle" to place Black girls' strengths, needs, and aspirations at the heart of your work, ensuring that your classroom becomes a space of growth and belonging.

THE BELIEF FRAMEWORK

As you read this book, you will likely develop many ideas for supporting Black girls in your educational setting. One powerful tool to help you turn these ideas into meaningful action is the BELIEF framework. The BELIEF framework can be used strategically to implement and measure specific practices, allowing you to track their impact on the learning environment, particularly for Black girls.

The framework is most effective when used on a larger scale—across multiple classrooms, schools, or within an organization—allowing for consistent implementation and evaluation. By using BELIEF, you can ensure that your practices are aligned with your goals for equity and student success, while also tracking progress over time to see what works and where adjustments may be needed.

With this framework, you'll be able to define your goals, apply evidence-based practices, and measure their impact in a structured way. This allows for a focused, collective effort to create a learning environment that is truly supportive and transformative for Black girls, fostering an atmosphere of success and growth.

The BELIEF framework is designed to guide educators and organizations through a process of intentional practice and reflection. The Conclusion provides more detail about this framework, but, for now, here's an overview of each part of the framework:

B – Begin With Belief

Start by cultivating a deep, unwavering belief in the potential of Black girls. This belief forms the foundation for all your practices, so you will also need to take time to re-familiarize yourself about who you believe you are in their lives. Do you believe that you are a change agent? Approach every interaction, decision, and initiative with the understanding that Black girls have the ability to succeed and thrive in any learning environment. This belief sets the tone for the work ahead and shapes the way you engage with students.

E – Envision Their Futures

Imagine the possibilities for Black girls and the futures you want them to have. Create a clear vision of success that includes academic achievement, personal growth, and social-emotional well-being. This vision will guide your efforts and help you maintain focus on the long-term goals. Envisioning their futures helps to build a sense of purpose and direction, ensuring that all actions align with the ultimate goal of student success.

L – Leverage Data

To effectively support Black girls, educators must make data-driven decisions. This involves reviewing a variety of relevant data, including academic performance, discipline records, attendance, and observational data. Additionally, it is crucial to gather anecdotal data directly from Black girls, listening to their experiences and understanding their most pressing needs. By analyzing these data, you can identify patterns, uncover barriers to success, and tailor their practices to address specific challenges. Leveraging data ensures that decisions are grounded in reality and that interventions are responsive and targeted to the unique needs of Black girls.

I – Implement Your Practices

Once your beliefs and vision are set and you understand the needs, gaps, and opportunities, it's time to implement your practices. This step is about turning your ideas into action. Whether it's through culturally responsive teaching, mentoring programs, affinity groups, or inclusive classroom practices, consistency in implementation is necessary. Ensure that these practices are applied equitably and effectively, creating an environment where Black girls feel supported and empowered to succeed.

E – Evaluate Your Efforts

Evaluation is essential for understanding the effectiveness of your practices. Collect and analyze both qualitative and quantitative data on how well the implemented strategies are meeting your goals. Regular evaluation allows you to make data-informed decisions, identify areas for improvement, and ensure that your practices are having a positive impact on the learning environment for Black girls.

F – Fortify Your Approaches

The final step is about sustaining and strengthening your practices over time. Use the insights gained from evaluation to refine and improve your approaches. This is an ongoing process that requires flexibility and adaptability, ensuring that your practices continue to meet the needs of Black girls as they evolve. Fortifying your approaches involves building a culture of continuous improvement, where both educators and students are supported in their growth and success.

Take your time with each chapter, reflecting as you go, and remember that this book is a tool—a means to better serve, understand, and advocate for each Black girl who steps into your learning space and classroom.

NOTES

1. Murray, P. (2017). *Girlhood interrupted: The erasure of Black girls' child-hood.* Georgetown Law Center on Poverty and Inequality. https://genderjusticeandopportunity.georgetown.edu/wp-content/uploads/2020/06/girlhood-interrupted.pdf

2. Goodenow, C. (1993). Classroom belonging among early adolescent students: Relationships to motivation and achievement. *Journal of Early Adolescence, 13*(1), 21–43. https://doi.org/10.1177/0272431693013001002

3. Ryan, R., & Deci, E. (2000). Self-determination theory and the facilitation of intrinsic motivation, social development, and well-being. *The American Psychologist, 55,* 68–78. https://doi.org/10.1037/0003-066X.55.1.68

4. Osterman, K. F. (2000). Students' need for belonging in the school community. *Review of Educational Research, 70*(3), 323–367. https://doi.org/10.2307/1170786

5. Walton, G. M., & Cohen, G. L. (2011). A brief social-belonging intervention improves academic and health outcomes of minority students. *Science, 331*(6023), 1447–1451. https://doi.org/10.1126/science.1198364

6. Major landmarks in the progress of African Americans in higher education. (n.d.). *Journal of Blacks in Higher Education.* Retrieved April 22, 2025, from https://jbhe.com/chronology/

7. Creekmore, B. B. (2018, October 9). Me4ut (Minority enrichment for the University of Tennessee). *Volopedia.* https://volopedia.lib.utk.edu/entries/me4ut-minority-enrichment-for-the-university-of-tennessee/

8. Carr, S. (2022, January 5). Why we could soon lose even more Black teachers. *The Hechinger Report.* https://hechingerreport.org/why-we-could-soon-lose-even-more-black-teachers/

9. Smith, T. (2023, January 10). *Teacher diversity in the classroom: Does exposure to same-race teachers help students in the long run?* American Economic Association. https://www.aeaweb.org/research/same-race-teachers-long-run

10. Perry, A. (2019, October 16). *For better student outcomes, hire more Black teachers.* Brookings. https://www.brookings.edu/articles/for-better-student-outcomes-hire-more-black-teachers/

11. Blake, J. J., & Epstein, R. (2019, May 14). Listening to Black women and girls: Lived experiences of adultification bias. *Georgetown Law Center on Poverty and Inequality.*

12. Blake, J. J., & Epstein, R. (2019, May 14). Listening to Black women and girls: Lived experiences of adultification bias. *Georgetown Law Center on Poverty and Inequality.*

13. Tatum, B. D. (1997). *"Why are all the Black kids sitting together in the cafeteria?" And other conversations about race.* Basic Books.

14. Neblett, E., Rivas-Drake, D., & Umaña-Taylor, A. (2012). The promise of racial and ethnic protective factors in promoting ethnic minority youth development. *Child Development Perspectives, 6,* 295–303.

15. Epstein, R., Blake, J., & González, T. (2017, June 27). *Girlhood interrupted: The erasure of Black girls' childhood.* Available at SSRN: http://dx.doi.org/10.2139/ssrn.3000695

PART 1

Reflect on Beliefs and Biases

The journey toward educational equity begins with an honest and often challenging exploration of our own beliefs. **Part 1: *Reflect* on Beliefs and Biases** invites you to pause and reflect—not to place blame or invoke sympathy but to increase awareness of the ways in which your beliefs, whether conscious or unconscious, shape your classroom practices. Part 1 of this book encourages you to look inward with curiosity and openness, not with guilt or shame. It's about recognizing that we all carry biases, but more importantly, it's about taking actionable steps to address them and ensure that Black girls in our classrooms have the opportunities they deserve to thrive.

Chapter 1: "It's Not My Fault; It Is My Problem" challenges us to understand that, while we may not be directly responsible for the systemic inequities that Black girls face in education, we are still part of the broader educational system that must change. This chapter encourages you to move beyond guilt or defensiveness and instead focus on how you, as an educator, can take responsibility for the impact you have on your students' experiences. The historical context provided here is meant to increase awareness—not to make you feel overwhelmed but to give you the tools and knowledge necessary to see where change is needed. By owning our role in this process, we become empowered to act, with the recognition that transformation begins within ourselves and our practices.

Chapter 2: "Practice One—Identify Your Beliefs" takes this self-exploration a step further by guiding you to reflect on your own beliefs and biases toward Black girls. This is not about labeling yourself as "good" or "bad." Instead, this chapter invites you to examine what you might unknowingly believe about Black girls based on societal stereotypes and how these beliefs can influence your classroom. Do you recognize their full potential and their strengths? This practice encourages you to reflect, question, and reframe those beliefs. It's not about perfection—it's about awareness and growth. The tools provided in this chapter will help you challenge any unconscious biases and move toward a deeper, more authentic understanding of each student as an individual. This process doesn't need to feel daunting; it's simply about becoming more aware and taking intentional steps toward better serving all students, particularly Black girls.

Throughout **Part 1**, you will be encouraged to engage in self-reflection with compassion, not judgment. The purpose is not to overwhelm or to assign blame but to foster a deeper understanding of how our beliefs shape the classroom environment. By increasing our awareness, we open the door to meaningful change. Remember, this process is about growth—taking one small step at a time. This section is an invitation to reflect, acknowledge, and move forward with a commitment to doing better. As you work through these chapters, it's important to recognize that this is a journey, not a destination, and the goal is not to be perfect but to be open, aware, and willing to change.

The process of reflection and self-awareness that you'll begin here is not easy, but it is absolutely essential for creating the kind of educational environment that Black girls deserve. The work ahead may feel challenging at times, but it is not about fault; rather, it's about progress. Each step you take toward understanding your beliefs and biases is a step toward creating a classroom where every student feels valued, supported, and empowered to reach their fullest potential. **Part 1** will help you lay that foundation, equipping you with the awareness and tools needed to transform your classroom and the lives of your students. The journey may not be simple, but it is a necessary and powerful one.

CHAPTER 1

It's Not My Fault; It Is My Problem

BLACK GIRLS' EDUCATIONAL EQUITY

Public education in the United States was not created with Black girls in mind. It was not created with any Black person in mind and certainly not a Black female person. Countless historical records from the 18th century prove this reality. At its inception, public education sought to develop competent citizens capable of maintaining and upholding a democracy that supported the earliest views of the U.S. Founding Fathers. The Founding Fathers believed that "preserving democracy would require an educated population that could understand political and social issues and would participate in civic life, vote wisely, protect their rights and freedoms, and resist tyrants and demagogues."[1] However, in the early days of the United States, education was treated as a privilege deliberately denied to individuals of African descent, reflecting the entrenched anti-Black mindset and exclusionary practices of the time. Restricted by law, enslaved persons of African descent were prohibited from receiving an education. The Georgia slave codes allowed for punishment, at the court's discretion, by fining or whipping an enslaved person if they were found reading, writing, or being taught to read or write.[2] Louisiana laws criminalized teaching slaves to read or write, punishable by death or a lifetime of hard labor. South Carolinian legislation even outlawed "mental meetings," which included reading, writing, arithmetic, and memorization. By the 1830s, all slave states except Maryland, Tennessee, and Kentucky had passed anti-literacy laws that prohibited enslaved persons or freed Black persons from teaching or learning to read or write.[3] Slave owners who held enslaved persons against their will shared concerns that literate enslaved persons could forge their travel passes.

Other slave owners feared that information sharing would lead to more slave rebellions. Slave revolts such as the 1739 Stono Rebellion and the 1831 Nat Turner revolt made anti-literacy an urgent implementation for systemic control of enslaved persons. White slave owners felt that Black persons with the ability to read and write could use their skills to create an imbalance in the power structure between master and slave. Literate persons of African descent threatened the way of life that justified slavery. All while the early American economy was being built on the backs of enslaved persons, reading and writing were no priority and had no place in slavery since enslaved persons were not viewed as more than property. However, learning to read and write revealed that this so-called "property" had a mind that challenged the idea that they were less than human. Learning to read and write revealed hope beyond the inhumanity enslaved persons were forced to experience. Literacy meant freedom—intellectual freedom until physical freedom could be realized. Black literacy was a revolutionizing weapon and the ultimate tool for enslaved persons to build, organize, and push toward freedom. This is the very reason white slave owners worked to forbid it.

As explored by Heather A. Williams in *Self-Taught: African American Education in Slavery*, enslaved persons took on many methods to acquire education, even against the laws governing early U.S. society. Enslaved persons knew the importance of education and valued it with as much worth as life itself. Slave narratives and memoirs have provided us with more insight into the punishments and efforts that white citizens used against Black literacy. Some years after escaping slavery, Gordon Buford, a former slave, recounted how he and other enslaved persons never learned to read because the slave owner threatened to "skin them alive" if they were ever caught doing so. When formerly enslaved Belle Caruthers's owner caught her reading a dictionary, he struck her down with his muddy boots. Other records recount how enslaved persons watched in horror when enslaved persons were hanged for teaching others to read.[4]

With each new law or punishment against learning, enslaved persons grew increasingly stealthy in spreading the skill of reading and writing. Black men and women worked together to ensure that literacy within the enslaved community remained a resolute commitment. Williams passionately states, "Understanding how enslaved people learned not only illuminates the importance of literacy as an instrument of resistance and liberation but also brings into view the clandestine tactics and strategies enslaved people employed to gain some control over their own lives."[5]

Gender-based labor roles significantly shaped the ways in which Black women and girls sought and obtained education during and after slavery. Enslaved Black women were assigned a range of labor roles that placed them in diverse environments—both domestic and agricultural. While many Black men and boys were primarily tasked with fieldwork, Black girls and women often worked in domestic roles within the slave owner's household, performing tasks such as cooking, cleaning, and caring for children.[6] This separation of labor, while gendered, meant that Black women and girls had more varied interactions with both enslavers and other enslaved people. For instance, those in domestic roles might have had more direct access to literacy practices, whether by overhearing lessons intended for the slave owner's children or observing their enslavers engage in reading and writing. In contrast, Black women and girls working in the fields were more likely to engage with communal and oral forms of knowledge, sharing survival strategies, history, and cultural practices through storytelling and conversation.

Williams highlights several accounts of enslaved Black girls and women learning to read from their white owners' children, who may not have been as knowledgeable about the anti-literacy laws, and accounts of Black women secretly carrying newspapers and books from their white slave owners' homes to teach themselves and other enslaved persons.

The onset of the Civil War in 1861 only encouraged the desire for Black literacy. Black enslaved persons were learning that the Civil War could end slavery, causing slave masters to grow increasingly nervous about how Black literacy would impact the slavery structures they trusted. The Northern states also held discomfort with Black literacy. When the 1831 Convention of Colored Men of the United States was held in Pennsylvania, its delegates, freed Black men and white abolitionists, proposed forming a college for freed Black men in New Haven, Connecticut. However, this idea was crushed by the white citizens of New Haven, with political leaders believing that a college for the Black population would be "incompatible" with their existence. The mayor of New Haven stated, "We will resist the establishment of this college in this place by every lawful means."[7] In 1833 Connecticut prohibited Black persons who were not inhabitants of the state from attending an abolitionist-run boarding school established in 1832 for free Black girls. The white residents would later burn the building to the ground.

While barriers to Black literacy continued to persist, public education began taking its earliest form in the late 19th century. By 1870, approximately 78% of all children between the ages of 5 and 14 were enrolled in elementary school.[8] This period also marked a shift in governance, as many states began to incorporate the responsibility for public education into their state constitutions. However, despite this increased emphasis on public education for all U.S. children, Black children were often excluded from these educational opportunities.

Following the abolition of slavery in 1865, Black individuals began to gain the legal right to education, as ratified by the Thirteenth, Fourteenth, and Fifteenth Amendments, which collectively aimed to extend citizenship and civil rights to formerly enslaved people. Despite these constitutional protections, Black children were still subjected to deeply segregated and underfunded schools, with inadequate facilities and resources.[9] These disparities persisted as Black communities faced significant resistance to integration and equal access to quality education, particularly in the Southern states where Jim Crow laws further institutionalized racial segregation in schools.

Even beyond the unequal access to quality education for Black persons was the unequal access for female students. Once widespread access to public school was gained for both Black girls and Black boys in the mid-19th century, following the end of slavery and the passage of the Fourteenth and Fifteenth Amendments, Black children were generally allowed access to education. However, girls were sometimes taught a different curriculum and had limited access to higher education.[10] Additionally, social constructs and norms about women's place in society pushed the importance of education for Black girls to the background. Although Black women and men were philosophically committed to education, entrenched gender roles imposed by society often relegated women to domestic responsibilities, making it harder for them to access education in the same way as men. The expectation that women should prioritize managing the home and raising children created significant barriers to their educational opportunities.

Still, the fight for equality, equity, and improved educational conditions for Black children pushed forward. The overturning of *Plessy v. Ferguson* by the 1954 *Brown v. Board of Education* ruling disrupted the idea of separate but equal conditions in American public schools. It led to historic changes in the learning experiences of Black and white students. As schools began desegregating, there were hopes that this new policy would correct the flawed educational system to one that was more equitable and just for Black children. Instead, the unintended consequences of closing Black schools, firing Black teachers, and demoting Black principals created a lack of trust in the intentions and goals of desegregated schools. The post–Civil Rights era of public education continues to find Black children inequitably served and disproportionately impacted.[11]

According to 2019 National Assessment of Educational Progress (NAEP) data, 82% of Black fourth graders scored below proficient in reading, and 87% of eighth graders scored below proficient in math.[12] Although still lower than that of white students, Black student achievement has shown minimal improvement in recent years, partly due to federal initiatives such as No Child Left Behind, Race to the Top, and My Brother's Keeper. The programs have sought to bring more attention and intention toward providing equitable support for Black students. These initiatives have optimistic hopes, and some have shown improvements in historically marginalized subgroups. However, they do not explicitly highlight the complexities associated with the intersectionality of race and gender, uniquely experienced by Black girls. According to the U.S. Government Accountability Office's (GAO)'s analysis of the most recent pre-pandemic Department of Education data, Black girls represented 15% of all girls in public schools during the 2017–2018 school year, yet they accounted for a disproportionately high share of school disciplinary measures. Nationally, they made up 45% of out-of-school suspensions, 37% of in-school suspensions, and 43% of expulsions. These punitive actions were frequently issued in response to subjective behaviors such as defiance, disrespect, and disruption—infractions for which Black girls were more harshly disciplined than their white peers across every U.S. state.[13]

There is an oversight of the intricacies that permeate Black girls' place in education. This oversight results from circumstances that first excluded Black persons and then Black girls from educationally centered conversations.

In recounting the history of Black persons' inability to experience the right to education in the United States, it should now be clearer why I say that public education was not created with Black people in mind. At every significant juncture in societal change in the United States, Black persons, especially girls, were excluded, pushed out, turned away, or limited from accessing education. From anti-literacy laws across the Southern states, restrictive access to education in the Northern states, the underserved conditions created by Jim Crow, and the neglect following the Civil Rights era, education for Black people in the United States has never been a priority. Therefore, it is evident that no systemic intentionality was placed on creating an educational system that truly serves Black people. As Professors Michael J. Dumas and Joseph Derrick Nelson shared in *(Re) Imagining Black Boyhood*, "beginning in slavery, Black boys and girls were imagined as chattel and were often put to work as young as two and three years old. Subject to much of the dehumanization suffered by Black adults, Black children were rarely perceived as worthy of playtime and were severely punished for exhibiting normal child-like behaviors."[14] Due to generations of racial injustice, we now have a functioning educational construct that seeks to serve all students yet was not created for all students. The only way we can improve such a system is to pick it apart, examine the experiences of every group impacted by this system, and work to intentionally create a system that values, uplifts, and creates belonging for each group. This is why it's crucial to reframe our thinking about what Black girls need in their educational environments. For individual teachers, this reframing means moving beyond a one-size-fits-all approach to recognizing the unique, nuanced needs of Black girls in the classroom. It requires understanding the historical context that shapes their educational experiences and actively working to create an environment where they are not just tolerated but celebrated. Black girls need spaces where their voices are heard, their cultural identities are respected, and their experiences are seen as valuable contributions to the learning community. They also need educators who are aware of and responsive to the impacts of implicit bias and systemic inequities that disproportionately affect them.

Teachers can create this environment by working through the practices referenced in the coming chapters, which involve integrating asset-based beliefs into the learning environment, fostering an atmosphere of respect and compassionate communication, and encouraging inclusive thinking around race, identity, and history. It also means providing opportunities for Black girls to engage in leadership roles, build strong mentorship relationships, and have access to emotional and social support within the school system.

Despite the disparities, Black girls and women persistently pursue spaces historically dominated by men or white women. This pursuit of achievement should come as no surprise. The desire for excellence, knowledge, and intellectual wealth has been passed through generations of Black people from ancient

African education principles. The African nation of Timbuktu served as an educational hub for its 25,000-student university from the 13th to 16th centuries.[15] And, while much of the discussions about the origins of science and math are focused on the Greek and Roman empires, it was the Yoruba people of modern-day Nigeria who developed a numeric system more than 8,000 years ago, the Dogon people of Mali who provided early astronomical studies about Jupiter and Saturn, the Tanzanian people who built furnaces that could reach temperatures much higher than those of the Romans, and the nations in modern-day Egypt, South Africa, and Nigeria who discovered the use of plants that contained salicylic acid (aspirin) for pain relief.[16] So, it should be no astonishment that Black people have continued pursuing education, knowledge, and economic sustenance. In ancient Africa, the roles and responsibilities of women in teaching and learning varied across different societies and cultures. In some societies, women played a significant role in teaching and passing down knowledge to the next generation. For example, in many African societies, women were responsible for teaching children and young people about the cultural traditions and values of the community. Women might also serve as mentors and role models for young people, providing guidance and support in their personal and educational development. Overall, the place of women in ancient African teaching and learning was shaped by the cultural, social, and historical context in which they lived, and the specific roles and responsibilities they held may have varied widely across different societies and cultures.

However, due to the systemic structure of racism and the unapologetic social construct of sexism, Black women have been diminished to a status unequivocally met with a double impact on the throes of racism and sexism. Economist Michelle Holder found that "approximately $50 billion of wages were involuntarily forfeited by Black women due to discriminatory employment practices."[17]

Black women remain significantly underrepresented in executive-level positions across industries in the United States. As of recent reports, Black women occupy only about 4% of C-suite roles in large corporations, a stark contrast to the 62% held by white men.[18] White women hold approximately 20% of executive positions, and men of color account for around 13%.[19] Despite representing a substantial portion of the workforce, Black women continue to face systemic barriers that hinder their advancement into top leadership roles. Although there has been some progress in increasing diversity in leadership positions, Black women still face significant challenges in reaching executive ranks.

Regarding advanced courses and college enrollment, Black women also face challenges. According to data from the National Center for Education Statistics (NCES), Black women represented approximately 11% of all undergraduate students in the United States during the 2019–2020 academic year. This is significantly lower compared to white women, who comprised 43% of the undergraduate student population, and white men, who made up 35%. These data highlight the underrepresentation of Black women in higher education when compared to other racial and gender groups.[20]

Black girls and women have either been dismissed from or pushed out of societal advancement, but they continue striving for achievement. As stated by Andre M. Perry, "the growing educational and cultural influence of Black women doesn't equal protection."[21] This protection and support begin by reexamining how educators show up for Black girls before they become Black women.

It is important to address the systemic and institutional barriers that contribute to the disparities faced by Black girls in education, as well as the broader implications of these challenges in shaping their future opportunities. By focusing on Black girls during middle school, a critical moment in both academic and social-emotional development, educators have the unique opportunity to intervene at a pivotal stage. This is a time when Black girls are navigating not only their academic identities but also their social and emotional growth, which is crucial for their overall well-being and future success. Supporting Black girls in these formative years is not just about helping them succeed in school—it is about creating a foundation for a more equitable future across various domains, including higher education, corporate settings, and beyond.

By actively working to dismantle the barriers that impede their success and creating educational spaces that protect and uplift Black girls academically and social-emotionally, we can begin to reverse the cycles of inequity that have long plagued this group. When Black girls are given the tools to excel, both intellectually and emotionally, they gain the resilience, confidence, and critical skills necessary to thrive in higher education and enter the workforce with the strength to challenge systemic barriers. This can lead to greater representation in leadership positions, a reduction in racial disparities in pay and employment opportunities, and a more inclusive, diverse future workforce.

The atrocities and injustices that have historically affected Black girls and women—ranging from limited access to quality education to being underrepresented in leadership roles—will begin to decline as we prioritize their success at the educational level. This work must start with an intentional focus on middle school, a time when Black girls are often at a crossroads. When educators provide support that is both academically rigorous and social-emotionally protective, we can pave the way for a generation of Black women who will have the confidence, skills, and opportunities to break down the barriers in higher education, corporate spaces, and other critical arenas.

CLAIMING THE PATH FORWARD

The systemic racism embedded in U.S. educational history has had a profound and lasting impact on the experiences of Black girls in American schools, excluding and marginalizing them from vital opportunities to learn and grow. Yet the struggle for education and equal opportunity has been relentless and courageous—and it goes on. Despite facing insurmountable odds and battling a society that questions their worth and competence, Black girls and women continue to pursue excellence, knowledge, and intellectual wealth.

To address these long-standing disparities and work toward the equitable and just educational system so many have fought for, we can and must undertake transformative practices that prioritize Black girls' experiences. It is crucial to create an educational environment that focuses on academic achievement, social-emotional well-being, and empowerment of Black girls. This requires a comprehensive approach that considers the intersectionality of race and gender, providing support and protection for Black girls' intellectual and personal growth.

Our collective responsibility is to recognize and embrace Black girls' potential, brilliance, and resilience and to invest in their future, build better educational experiences, and dismantle the systemic barriers that have hindered their progress for far too long. Only through intentional and transformative practices can we create a space in our educational system that values, uplifts, and ensures belonging for every student, regardless of their background or identity.

In this way, we honor the legacy of those who have fought for educational equity and justice for Black girls throughout history. We must continue their work and strive for a future where every Black girl has the opportunity to flourish and reach her full potential, contributing to the advancement of our society. The time for change is now, and educators, policymakers, and communities are responsible for ensuring that our educational system truly serves all students.

Taking responsibility for this work is hard, but it's essential. I'm going to give you the means to undertake it and then, together, we'll do it. In the next chapters, you will find five key practices that will serve as tools to guide you in this journey. These practices are designed to equip you with the strategies and actions you need to make a meaningful impact. The work ahead will require dedication, self-reflection, and a willingness to challenge existing systems, but with these practices, you will have the foundation to transform the environments you work in and create lasting change. This journey is not easy, but it is possible, and I am here to support you every step of the way.

In the Middle

Honoring History, Empowering the Future—A
Reflection on Black Girls' Educational Equity

In this chapter, you were introduced to the historical context of Black people's early educational experiences in America, particularly Black women. The reflections below are designed to help you deepen your understanding and consider how this history informs your current teaching practice. As you engage with these questions, reflect honestly on your personal experiences, biases, and the steps you can take to foster a more equitable learning environment for Black girls.

> **Reflect Deeply**. Take a moment to consider what you've learned about the early educational experiences of Black people and how systemic barriers have shaped Black girls' education.

> **Be Specific**. When answering, draw on examples from your teaching practice or observations.

Your reflections are an opportunity to deepen your understanding of Black girls' educational experiences and consider small, meaningful steps you can take to create a more inclusive and supportive classroom. This isn't about having all the answers; rather, it's about learning, growing, and making progress one step at a time.

REFLECTION QUESTIONS

1. What is something that you did not know and have now learned about the early education experiences of Black people, particularly Black women in America?

2. How do you think these systemic experiences have influenced the Black girls you know or interact with in your school?

This reflection will help you connect historical context to the real, everyday experiences of the students in your care, guiding you toward more thoughtful and supportive practices.

NOTES

1. Kober, N., & Rentner, D. S. (2020). *History and evolution of public education in the US*. George Washington University, Center on Education Policy. https://files.eric.ed.gov/fulltext/ED606970.pdf

2. Georgia Archives University System of Georgia. (n.d.). *Slave laws of Georgia, 1755-1860*. https://www.georgiaarchives.org/assets/documents/Slave_Laws_of_Georgia_1755-1860.pdf

3. Smithsonian American Art Museum. (n.d.). *Literacy as freedom*. https://americanexperience.si.edu/wp-content/uploads/2014/09/Literacy-as-Freedom.pdf

4. Williams, H. A. (2008). *Self-taught: African American education in slavery and freedom*. University of North Carolina Press.

5. Williams, H. A. (2008). *Self-taught: African American education in slavery and freedom*. University of North Carolina Press, p. iv.

6. White, D. G. (1999). *Ar'n't I a Woman? Female slaves in the plantation South*. Norton.

7. Cromwell, W. J. (2020). *The new Negroes and the New York renaissance*. University of Georgia Press, p. 14.

8. Neem, J. N. (2017). *Democracy's schools: The rise of public education in America*. Johns Hopkins University Press, p. 177.

9. Rury, J. L. (2013). *Education and social change: Contours in the history of American schooling* (4th ed.). Routledge.

10. Kober, N., & Rentner, D. S. (2020). *History and evolution of public education in the US*. George Washington University, Center on Education Policy. https://files.eric.ed.gov/fulltext/ED606970.pdf

11. Ricks, S. A. (2014). Falling through the cracks: Black girls and education. *Journal of Teaching and Learning*, 4, 10–21.

12. National Center for Education Statistics. (2019, October 30). *2019 NAEP mathematics and reading assessments: Highlighted results at grades 4 and 8 for the nation, states, and districts* (NCES Publication No. 2020-012). U.S. Department of Education. https://nces.ed.gov/pubsearch/pubsinfo.asp?pubid=2020012

13. U.S. Government Accountability Office. (2024, September 10). *K-12 education: Nationally, Black girls receive more frequent and more severe discipline in school than other girls* (GAO-24-106787). https://www.gao.gov/assets/gao-24-106787.pdf

14. Epstein, R., Blake, J., & González, T. (2017, June 27). *Girlhood interrupted: The erasure of Black girls' childhood*. Available at SSRN: http://dx.doi.org/10.2139/ssrn.3000695

15. Timbuktu: Home of Sankoré University. (2016). *Journal of Pan African Studies (Online)*, 9(9), 269–271.

16. Blatch, S. (2013, February 1). *Great achievements in science and technology in Ancient Africa.* American Society for Biochemistry and Molecular Biology. https://www.asbmb.org/asbmb-today/science/020113/great-achievements-in-stem-in-ancient-africa

17. Holder, M. (2022, March 31). *The "double gap" and the bottom line: African American women's wage gap and corporate profits.* Roosevelt Institute. https://rooseveltinstitute.org/publications/the-double-gap-and-the-bottom-line-african-american-womens-wage-gap-and-corporate-profits/

18. Rhodes, D. (2024, February 8). *Black women in the C-suite.* Women Business Collaborative. https://wbcollaborative.org/insights/black-women-in-the-c-suite/

19. Zippia. (2023, June 8). *25 women in leadership statistics [2023]: Facts on the gender gap in corporate and political leadership.* Zippia.com. https://www.zippia.com/advice/women-in-leadership-statistics/

20. National Center for Education Statistics. (2020). *Enrollment of women in postsecondary education.* U.S. Department of Education, Institute of Education Sciences. https://nces.ed.gov/fastfacts/display.asp?id=98

21. Perry, A. M. (2020, July). *To protect black women and save America from itself, elect Black women.* Brookings. https://www.brookings.edu/articles/to-protect-black-women-and-save-america-from-itself-elect-black-women/

CHAPTER 2

Practice
One—Identify
Your Beliefs

> *"Our Black girls need us to see them and to recognize their curiosity, independence, and discontent, not to assume they are combative and angry without reason."*
>
> — Monique W. Morris

I have dedicated my career to serving underrepresented communities. While I have always taught in urban schools with high populations of Black students, I have always been one of the few Black teachers in the school building. In my first year of teaching, I remember two of my white colleagues expressing that their first time being in an extended presence with a Black girl was as a teacher at our school, not during their upbringing as kids, not in their collegiate programs, and not during their student teaching year. There are a host of reasons why that was the case. Perhaps because, as a young student, my white colleagues grew up in a community with few people of color, with few or no Black people. Perhaps it is because, in their college journey, they attended an institution with few people of color enrolled. Over the past two decades, the college enrollment rate for Black students initially showed an upward trend, but it has recently declined. This shift is particularly evident in a drop in enrollment at community colleges and a stagnation in attendance at highly selective universities, leading to a decrease in overall college participation for Black students compared to earlier years. Data from Hanson highlights the racial disparity in college enrollment, showing that in 2022, 41% of white 18- to 24-year-olds were enrolled in college, compared to just 36% of Black students, underscoring the persistent gap in higher education access.[1] It's crucial to remember that this disparity in college enrollment isn't just a result of academic success gaps, as Black students have been found to outperform white students on standardized examinations. Family income, which affects access to quality child care, enrichment activities, and educational resources, plays a significant role in shaping student outcomes, with research showing that when family income disparities are accounted for, the racial test score gap often narrows or even reverses, as seen in studies where Black students outperform white students on early assessments.[2] Discrimination, systemic educational hurdles, unequal access to resources and opportunity, and other socioeconomic factors have most certainly contributed to these statistics.

Also, it is possible that during my white colleagues' student teaching year, there was no focus or priority on ensuring they were placed in a classroom environment that would mimic the cultural, racial, or ethnic diversity experience as an in-service teacher. This lack of diverse placements in teacher preparation programs can result in teachers being unprepared to effectively engage with students from different racial, cultural, and ethnic backgrounds, which is critical for fostering an inclusive and equitable classroom environment.[3] In thinking of all the reasons why my colleagues had not had the privilege of teaching or even knowing a Black girl, I also could not help but wonder, *What do they believe about Black girls? What assumptions, biases, and perceptions might they hold, even unconsciously?* As they shared their thoughts openly with me, I began to reflect on this question: What are the first thoughts that come to their minds when my white colleagues see a Black girl sitting in their class? Some might insist, "Of course, they see a student ready to learn, just like any other student." While some may speak with passion, humility, and truth, it is essential to acknowledge that color-blindness is not a neutral stance—it is a harmful trope that denies the lived experiences and identities of Black girls and, in fact, can perpetuate racism. By disregarding their racial identity, we ignore the unique challenges Black girls face, such as discrimination and stereotyping, which shape their academic and social experiences. We must ask ourselves, *In failing to recognize the racial and gendered realities of their existence, are we reinforcing biases that impact their opportunities and experiences in the classroom?*

The history of brownness runs deep, shaping every aspect of what it means to be a Black girl. This history, however, stretches far beyond my own experiences as a young Black girl. It is rooted in the lived realities of generations before me— my mother's experiences as a Black woman during the Civil Rights movement, my grandmother's experiences in the early 1900s, my great-grandmother's during the Reconstruction Era, and my great-great-grandmother's during slavery. These lived histories—filled with trauma, resilience, and the quest for peace—are inextricably tied to who I am today. This identity, built upon centuries of racial and gendered experiences, began long before I existed, and it is far too complex to be reduced or ignored. Yet, when people encounter Black girls like me, this identity is often underexplained, underanalyzed, or even completely overlooked. Such neglect leads to assumptions that disregard the profound, generational history behind who we are. Refusing to recognize the racial identity of Black girls is not only an act of erasure but also a refusal to acknowledge something fundamental that cannot be hidden or discarded. My identity as a Black woman, shaped by these generations, explains why I enter spaces with a predefined confidence, despite the stereotypes and biases that attempt to define me. It took time and struggle to trust that my sense of self was not shaped by the narrow assumptions of others. What I am describing here is the word "bias," which often misrepresents or distorts who people truly are.

If you are an educator reading this, you have undoubtedly encountered the word "bias" in professional development workshops. In its simplest form, bias refers to holding an opinion or making a judgment about something before fully understanding the facts. One specific type of bias, implicit bias, plays a crucial role in how we perceive and interact with others, often without conscious awareness. Implicit bias involves the attitudes or stereotypes that affect our understanding, actions, and decisions in an unconscious manner. It can manifest in subtle ways, such as unintentionally favoring one group of students over another. In my conversation with my colleagues, I found myself wondering what assumptions they might hold about Black girls in their classrooms. Given that no one can ever truly "spend enough time" with an entire racial group to fully understand the complexities of their experiences, it struck me that these assumptions were likely shaped by incomplete or biased perceptions. Implicit bias often leads to these types of misjudgments, where people unknowingly form conclusions based on stereotypes. Recognizing and addressing implicit bias is a crucial step toward fostering a more inclusive and equitable learning environment for all students.

Let me ease things for you before you close this book and decide that it's another book telling you what you're doing is wrong. The truth is that we all have biases. As my white colleagues shared their lack of perspective about the Black girls in their classrooms, I was forming a bias about my colleagues that perhaps they did not have a good working knowledge about how to interact with children from differing cultural or ethnic backgrounds. I could not help but continue to wonder, *If my colleagues have never been around Black girls, are they able to teach Black children and nurture our Black girls?* I know what you're probably thinking—how dare she think that? Any teacher can teach any student! I know. I know. The fact that I am sharing the biases I was developing is a massive vulnerability for me. Was I leaning toward the incorrect side of the facts about my colleagues? Perhaps I was. I can say that these colleagues have become close friends of mine over the years, and we have openly shared our early assumptions about several things in culture and specifically education. But my point is to show you that we all indeed have biases that can be formed from one encounter, one statement, one assumption.

The danger with biases, particularly those directed at Black girls, is that they can lead to harmful assumptions and behaviors that impact their well-being and success. These biases don't exist in isolation—Black girls face the intersection of both racial and gender biases, which can compound the negative effects they experience. This intersectionality amplifies the dangers, as these overlapping stereotypes often lead to more frequent and more intense misjudgments. For instance, while racial bias may assume that Black girls are less capable or less deserving of opportunities, gender bias might reinforce stereotypes of aggression or invisibility, further limiting their potential. As a result, Black girls are not only subject to external biases, but they also begin to internalize these perceptions as they form their ethnic-racial identity. This process can lead to feelings of self-doubt and reinforce the harmful stereotypes imposed upon them. In fact, the concept of **stereotype threat**—the fear of confirming negative stereotypes about one's social group—may be an important factor here, as Black girls may feel pressure to act or perform in ways that contradict their authentic selves to avoid reinforcing these stereotypes. Understanding these complexities is essential to creating a more supportive and equitable environment for Black girls, where they can thrive without the weight of societal assumptions shaping their identity.

What if I told you that, as an educator, you hold significant influence over how Black girls perceive themselves? Their understanding of their identity, especially within the academic realm, is deeply shaped by how you—both as a teacher and as an educational leader—view them. It's easy to assume that educators understand their responsibility to foster a positive and supportive learning environment, but how often do we pause to examine how our biases and beliefs might impact students, particularly Black girls? When you think of a Black girl in your class, where does your mind go? What assumptions, conscious or unconscious, influence your actions and expectations? This is not just a philosophical question; it's a practical one that shapes students' experiences in the classroom.

In my experience, while many educators might acknowledge the importance of equitable treatment and the impact they can have, they don't always confront these responsibilities head-on. It's not just about knowing; it's about truly engaging with the implications of those beliefs. And perhaps it's not just about school, either. Black girls' academic journey is shaped by the broader societal narrative that influences their sense of belonging and potential. We'll explore this further as we dive into research on Black girls and the stereotypes that have been imposed on them.

PAUSE FOR REFLECTION

As you read through this, take a moment to think about the Black girls in your classroom. Ask yourself, What assumptions do I hold about Black girls' behaviors, abilities, or potential? Are there moments when I notice myself feeling uncomfortable or challenged by a Black girl's actions or words? Why might that be? How have my own personal beliefs influenced how I interact with Black girls in the classroom?

UNPACKING EXPERIENCES: THE RESEARCH ON BLACK GIRLS AND THE IMPACT OF SOCIETAL BIAS

To suggest that educators must pause and think about what they believe about Black girls also means that there is an issue with the beliefs about Black girls. "Teacher/educator" belief is a concern not only for Black girls but for Black students in general. The "belief gap" refers to the phenomenon in which some educators lack belief in the potential of students from low-income backgrounds and students of color, often driven by negative stereotypes that go unchallenged within schools.[4] The "belief gap," understandably, can have detrimental effects on students of color, including decreased academic achievement and diminished self-confidence. Add the complexities of being a girl in this context, and there appears the bias that Black girls face.

This book is premised on the fact that Black girls do not get the same attention as other student groups. In fact, it is thought that researchers, activists, policymakers, and funders rarely devote their entire attention to the vulnerabilities that Black and other girls of color face.[5] In sifting through the educational research that does exist about perceptions, assumptions, biases, and beliefs about Black girls, I have been able to identify some key studies that support the necessity for more attention to the experiences of Black girls in school. As you read through my synopsis of these studies, I encourage you to continue thinking about the question asked earlier: *What do **you** believe about Black girls?*

STUDY 1

The qualitative study, *The Impossibility of Being "Perfect and White,"* conducted by four Black women researchers, explores how Black girls perceive and interpret their schooling experiences through racial and gendered lenses, while emphasizing the importance of conversation spaces that facilitate their critical reflection on both individual and collective educational experiences.[6]

But before we dig into the findings, first, check out that title. Does it lay on your chest a bit? It should. If you are a person of color reading this, then you understand the title all too well. When I came across this study, I read the title three times before entering the findings. I recalled being in elementary, middle, and even high school and listening to my teacher call out those students demonstrating behavior the teacher deemed "appropriate" to get the entire class to demonstrate this "appropriate" behavior. Behaviors like sitting in an "appropriate" way, speaking in an "appropriate" tone, dressing "appropriately," and asking and answering questions "appropriately." This positive reinforcement strategy is a common strategy used by teachers. But have you asked yourself who determines what is appropriate? Without conscious effort, it can be a harmful comparison approach that sends the message of behavior correction through the lens of implicit bias. This bias speaks to cultural assimilation as acceptable behavior. I have witnessed this strategy used in ways that highlight the acceptable behavior, but that behavior was typically demonstrated by a white student—specifically, a white girl.

If you are white and feeling uncomfortable, that's completely normal, and I encourage you to continue reading. Many accounts highlight how disciplinary policies and behavior management strategies can inadvertently erase cultural considerations, attempting instead to align students' behavior with norms rooted in whiteness. While I do not suggest that teachers are consciously creating these environments, it's important to recognize that systemic racism is embedded in the structures and policies of our educational system (as discussed in the Introduction). This manifests through microaggressions, cultural assimilation pressures, and colorblindness—ideas that reinforce the notion that "whiteness is right." These challenges further emphasize the need to critically examine our classroom practices. However, this process cannot begin until we confront our own biases and deeply held belief systems, acknowledging them and working to overcome them through intentional reflection and action.

The study also highlighted how conversation spaces for Black girls can improve their experiences. One of the essential questions that the researchers sought to answer was *How do Black girls describe and understand their school experiences as racialized and gendered?* The researchers conducted this study as an extension of a state project that sought to support school leaders with identifying efforts to improve Black students' academic achievement. In examining the data from the initial study, the researchers realized that there is more to be discovered regarding Black girls' experiences in schools. Through structured conversations at five public high schools and in group sizes ranging from 9 to 19 at each site, Black girl students engaged in dialogue to describe and interpret their racialized and gendered school experiences. The researchers' findings, summarized in the next section, revealed five attitudes and treatments that impact Black girls: *Notions of Femininity, Policing and Surveillance of Black Girl Bodies, Black Girls and (Anti)Intellectualism, Marginalization of Black Female Athletes, Black Girls in Relational Contexts,* and *Necessary Support Structures for Black Girls.*

NOTIONS OF FEMININITY

The expectations placed on Black girls to conform to narrow definitions of femininity are often reinforced through explicit comments from adults. For example, one girl shared, "If you just do one wrong thing, they'll be like, 'You're a lady, you weren't supposed to do that!' But everybody makes mistakes," highlighting how even minor deviations are harshly judged.

POLICING AND SURVEILLANCE OF BLACK GIRL BODIES

The hypersexualization of Black girls' clothing choices often leads to stricter disciplinary actions compared to their white peers. One student expressed frustration over this double standard, stating, "I'll be sent to the office for a coat, rain boots, and a pair of overalls that's two times my size . . . but Sally's gonna go learn and get the A+, while I'm stuck with a B because my knees are showing, which [with sarcasm] are very sexual, obviously." This reveals how policing their bodies disrupts their learning and reinforces inequities.

BLACK GIRLS AND (ANTI)INTELLECTUALISM

Black girls in schools often face both racial and gendered biases that diminish their intellectual potential. A student highlighted this stereotype, stating, "[A] lot of white people and people who aren't Black don't think that we know how to use our brains . . . so they have low expectations." This perception not only undermines their academic efforts but also perpetuates systemic inequities in educational opportunities and expectations.

MARGINALIZATION OF BLACK FEMALE ATHLETES

Black female athletes often encounter racialized and gendered bias in high school sports, leading to feelings of exclusion and invalidation. A student reflected on this disparity, saying, "Women's sports get no support moneywise, none at all . . . [teachers] will announce, 'Congratulations to the boys team,' but they won't say if [the girls] won a trophy or anything." This lack of recognition and support highlights how systemic inequities in sports mirror broader societal biases, undermining Black girls' value and contributions as athletes.

BLACK GIRLS IN RELATIONAL CONTEXTS

Black girls often experience complex social dynamics marked by competition, jealousy, and emotional intensity within their peer relationships. One participant shared, "We know we should have each other's backs, but it's hard when everyone's always trying to one-up each other, and things just get out of hand."

NECESSARY SUPPORT
STRUCTURES FOR BLACK GIRLS

Support structures such as other mothering and warm demander pedagogy were crucial for Black girls navigating challenges in their schools, as they provided mentorship, affirmation, and high expectations. One student reflected on the impact of her teacher, saying, "Ms. J is like a big mom to everybody, she just wants the best for us . . . she keeps it real with everybody."

Overall, the study highlights the need for schools to address the unique challenges Black girls face and create more inclusive and supportive environments for them. This may involve addressing negative stereotypes, promoting cultural competence among teachers and staff, and providing more resources and support for Black girls.

STUDY 2

"'They Told Me What I Was Before I Could Tell Them What I Was': Black Girls' Ethnic-Racial Identity Development Within Multiple Worlds" is a research article examining Black girls' ethnic-racial identity development in the United States.[7] The study is based on in-depth interviews with Black girls aged 12 to 18 and their parents, and it explores the various social, cultural, and historical factors that shape their identity. The article highlights how Black girls navigate and negotiate their identities within multiple worlds, including their families, communities, schools, and broader society. It also discusses the impact of racism and discrimination on their identity development and the role of resilience in helping them navigate these challenges.

Perhaps one of the most staunchly rich findings is the Black girl interviewees' perceptions of their race in social contexts. The girls' definitions of race were grounded in their social realities, with some referring to specific, observable physical attributes and others referring to cultural and socioeconomic stereotypical characteristics. For example, Desiree said being Black meant having darker skin but also living in a "bad" neighborhood. Terry described how there are two types of Black at her school: "African one" and "Ghetto." Aaliyah said she felt like her peers made assumptions about her race that made her "uncomfortable." Aaliyah also described being African American as "something people don't like" and associated with violence and ghetto stereotypes. Only two girls in the class provided positive beliefs and attitudes about their own ethnic-racial identities.

This study also highlights the surprising understanding of how differently Black girls defined race and what it meant to be of their race. While Black girls' conceptions of race tended to emphasize more tangible concepts, like physical appearance, their understanding of themselves tended to emphasize inter-actions within their societal domains and microsystems. The researchers contend that it is crucial to distinguish between students' understanding of the term "race" and how they apply it to their own lives. The high proportion of Black girls who spoke about embarrassing social encounters because of their ethnicity suggests that social experiences are crucial for shaping Black girls' early adolescent self-perceptions. The study concludes by discussing the implications of these findings for supporting the healthy development of Black girls and promoting a more inclu-sive and equitable society.

The study sheds light on the often-painful realities of Black girls' ethnic-racial identity development, illustrating how they are forced to navigate multiple worlds, each with its own set of expectations and stereotypes. As I reflect on these findings, I am reminded of my own experiences working in diverse educational settings, where Black students are con-stantly negotiating their identities in the face of societal judgments. Like the girls in the study, many of the students I've worked with have had to confront assumptions about their race, sometimes from peers who have little under-standing of their lived realities.

The findings of each of these studies reinforce what I've observed in my own career: the deep need for educators and leaders to not only be aware of the challenges Black students face but also create spaces where they feel empowered to define themselves outside the constraints of these limiting stereo-types. It's about offering more than just academic support; it's about fostering an environment that respects and nurtures their cultural identities, allowing them to develop into strong, resil-ient individuals. These studies call for a shift in how we think about race and identity in educational spaces—moving from a place of deficit and discomfort to one of celebration and affir-mation. It's time to provide Black girls with the space to truly understand and embrace who they are, free from the weight of others' misconceptions.

UNVEILING BELIEFS: A PATH TO EMPOWERMENT

In the journey to build better educational experiences for Black girls, it becomes evident that transformative practices are essential for educators. This chapter illuminates the need for a crucial starting point: *identifying our beliefs*.

The reflections within this chapter have unveiled the glaring gap in understanding that some educators may have about Black girls. In some cases, educators may not have had meaningful interactions with Black girls throughout their lives, and this lack of exposure can lead to biases and assumptions. The underlying premise is that acknowledging these biases is the first step toward dismantling them. We all harbor biases, often shaped by our limited exposure and cultural contexts, as noted previously by my own bias that I had to dismantle. It's not about pointing fingers but about self-awareness and growth. By recognizing that biases exist, educators can actively work toward creating inclusive and equitable learning environments for Black girls. This can involve seeking diverse perspectives, engaging in professional development on cultural competency, and fostering open dialogue with students to address misconceptions or stereotypes. Ultimately, educators can better support the success and well-being of Black girls in the education system through continuous self-reflection and a commitment to unlearning biases.

The research and studies shared in this chapter further emphasize the necessity of this work. Black girls face unique challenges in the educational system, including negative stereotypes, differential treatment, and a lack of inclusivity. The "belief gap" revealed in educational settings highlights how educators' biases can adversely affect Black students'—and especially Black girls'—experiences, leading to diminished self-confidence and academic achievement.

The path forward requires ongoing individual reflection and collective/system action. It's about acknowledging our biases and actively working to de-bias ourselves. The practice of identifying our beliefs about Black girls is about building a more inclusive and equitable educational environment.

THE WORK BEGINS

A central point connects each of these studies. The way that Black girls perceive themselves, experience school, and comprehend their place in society is primarily influenced by their everyday interactions with both peers and adults ("Perfect and White").

So, now what? What's next? Now, we actively work to challenge the biases against Black girls and create belief systems built on positive framing about their capabilities. What I will not be suggesting is another whole staff, schoolwide diversity training—this will not do much for changing deep-rooted biases—nor will I suggest another awkward cross-racial circle where everyone is asked to express their feelings about racism in the school but instead people of color end up educating their white colleagues about the stereotypes or biases experienced daily. No, not this time. This time, the work must be completely individual. Now is the time to look inward for those biases and then push outward for a belief system that drives one's attitude toward Black girls' experiences in school, contributing to a positive vision for Black girls' academic and social outcomes. All of this is to say that it is time to tear down the bias wall against our Black girls by tackling educators' personal belief systems first.

In this area, I've found value in the work of University of Wisconsin—Madison scholar and researcher Dr. Patricia Devine. She proposes, first and foremost, that bias is a habit—a learned behavior that becomes automatic and unconscious over time. Like any other unconscious behavior, it can be difficult to change, but it is possible to break the habit. To achieve this essential process of dismantling one's bias, Dr. Devine suggests three conditions that must exist individually: the intentional acknowledgment that biases exist, attention to triggers that influence stereotypical responses, and an investment of time to practice strategies that disrupt automatic or habitual assumptions about someone who is culturally or ethnically different.[8] Once these conditions are in place, it is possible to begin working to "de-bias."

Dr. Devine and her colleagues developed a program focused on multiple approaches to reducing implicit bias and breaking prejudice habits, including the following:

- **Individuation** means getting to know people as individuals instead of making assumptions based on the group they belong to.

  Example: If someone assumes that all employees from a certain background are shy, individuation will involve talking to each employee to learn about their unique qualities. For instance, by asking questions and getting to know them better, they might discover that one employee is very outgoing, which helps break the stereotype and see that person as an individual, not just part of a group.

- **Stereotype replacement** is a reassociation technique that encourage individuals to reevaluate their biases and consider alternative perspectives.

  Example: A simple reassociation exercise might ask participants to think of positive qualities or successful examples of people from a group they have biased assumptions about. For example, if someone holds a stereotype about young people from low-income backgrounds, they might be encouraged to think of successful individuals who have come from those environments, thus helping to break down the bias.

- **Counter-stereotyping** involves exposing individuals to counter-stereotypical information and examples to challenge their preconceived notions about certain groups of people.

  Example: In this approach, a participant might be shown stories or images of women excelling in fields traditionally dominated by men, such as engineering or technology. By encountering these counter-stereotypical examples, the individual's biases about women in these fields can be challenged and disrupted.

- **Increasing opportunities for contact** is an approach that involves bringing individuals from different groups together in a positive and supportive environment to foster understanding and reduce bias.

  Example: A group of individuals from different racial or cultural backgrounds might participate in a shared community project, such as volunteering at a local food bank. This collaborative setting allows participants to interact and get to know each other as individuals, building empathy and reducing the impact of biases they may have had previously.

- **Perspective taking** means trying to see things from the point of view of someone from a stereotyped group. This helps reduce automatic judgments based on group membership.

  Example: Imagine a teacher trying to understand what it's like to be a student from a different background. By thinking about the challenges that student might face, like being misunderstood or facing prejudice, the teacher can better empathize and respond with more fairness, rather than relying on stereotypes.

These same approaches can apply to educators' work moving from deficit to strengths-based mindsets. This work ultimately leads to a belief system that allows academic and social-emotional safety for Black girls.

It is unreasonable to expect to do this work in one day, with one book on one reflection page. De-biasing, reframing perspectives, and dismantling stereotypes is a lifetime journey. It requires ongoing effort and self-reflection to identify and address biases. I will say that the educators who support Black girls do not have the luxury to postpone this work. There must be a beginning, and that can be today.

On the reflection page "In the Middle: Identify Your Beliefs," you will first think through some approaches and considerations for disrupting bias and then apply the approach to biases about Black girls. You will then begin to build a positive belief system about Black girls. This belief system will fuel your vision and will certainly shape the culture and climate of your classroom and school building.

If we want to transform Black girls' experiences in school, it is a necessary step for educators to do the work to constantly crush biases and identify their strengths-based beliefs about Black girls to cultivate better outcomes.

In the Middle

Identify Your Beliefs

In this chapter, you explored the stereotypes and biases that Black girls face in educational settings, particularly how these biases shape their identities and experiences. The reflections below are designed to help you examine your own beliefs and how they influence your interactions with Black girls in the classroom. As you engage with these questions, reflect honestly on your perceptions, the biases you may hold, and the strategies you can implement to create a more supportive, inclusive, and empowering learning environment for Black girls.

REFLECTION TASK

The concept of de-biasing and reducing implicit bias can be applied to educators' work in developing strengths-based beliefs about Black girls.

In the space below, you will use one of these approaches to begin this work.

Reassociation: Black girls have often been on the receiving end of biased descriptors such as angry, disrespectful, loud, aggressive, feisty, mean, insecure, and lazy. Reframe these negative associations into positive affirming statements about Black girls.

Example: *Black girls are lazy.* Reframe: *Black girls are working to build hope.*

_____

_____

_____

Belief Statement: Now that you have developed positive, affirming statements about Black girls, transfer these statements into a belief statement about the Black girls you impact.

Sentence Starter: *I believe the Black girls I teach are . . .*

_____

_____

_____

Keep Doing the Work: How will you allow your actions to communicate your strengths-based beliefs about Black girls?

_____

_____

_____

Unseen Bias

A Teacher's Wake-up Call

Ms. Thompson had always prided herself on her deep love for teaching and her commitment to seeing each of her students as an individual. She had a special connection with Kayla, a bright Black girl in her class whom she often encouraged to be "tougher" in the face of challenges. Ms. Thompson saw so much potential in Kayla and often found herself thinking of her as a leader-in-the-making. She thought she was preparing Kayla for the world outside, believing that Black girls needed to be stronger to survive. But one day, Kayla pulled her aside after class.

"Ms. Thompson, when you said I needed to be tougher, it felt like you didn't think I was strong enough already," Kayla said, her voice soft but firm. "I don't hear you saying that to other girls. It's like you expect me to be different. But I don't get why."

A heavy silence filled the room. Ms. Thompson's heart sank as she realized the impact of her words. She had always believed she was helping Kayla, preparing her for challenges that Black girls like her would face. She had never considered how her well-meaning advice might be rooted in assumptions—biases—that she hadn't even recognized. She had unintentionally reinforced a stereotype, one that suggested Black girls had to be tougher, more resilient, less vulnerable, simply because of their racial identity.

"I'm so sorry, Kayla," Ms. Thompson said, her voice trembling. "I never meant to make you feel like that. I didn't mean to hurt you. I thought I was helping you be ready for the world. But I see now that I was basing that on only a small view of what I know about what you might need."

It wasn't just that Kayla felt hurt—it was that, for so long, Ms. Thompson had unconsciously bought into the very stereotypes she thought she was immune to. She had assumed that Black girls, especially, needed to be tougher, more independent, and more resilient to survive in the world. She hadn't seen how those assumptions could leave her students feeling unseen, misunderstood, or, worse, as if they had to carry a burden of strength that wasn't theirs to bear.

"I'm really grateful that you told me, Kayla," Ms. Thompson continued, her voice sincere. "You didn't have to speak up, but I'm so glad you did. I've learned something important today, and I promise to do better. I want you to know that you don't have to be anything but yourself. You are more than enough just as you are."

As Kayla smiled, the weight on Ms. Thompson's chest didn't lift immediately. The realization that she had unintentionally contributed to the very stereotypes she had worked so hard to avoid was painful. But it also marked a turning point in her teaching journey. She knew now that this was the beginning of a deeper reflection on her own biases—of the ways in which even the most well-intentioned beliefs can reinforce harmful ideas about Black girls.

From that day on, Ms. Thompson worked harder to examine her assumptions and actions. She educated herself about the challenges that Black girls face in education, attended workshops on culturally responsive teaching, and sought feedback from her Black students to make sure she was truly seeing them for who they were—without the weight of stereotypes or bias. She learned that teaching her students to be resilient didn't mean expecting them to bear a burden they didn't have to. Instead, it meant helping them embrace their authentic selves, giving them the space and support they needed to thrive, exactly as they were.

And while she couldn't erase the past, Ms. Thompson was committed to being a better teacher—not just for Kayla, but for every student who walked through her door. A teacher who understood that loving her students meant challenging her own biases, too.

NOTES

1. Hanson, M. (2024, August 31). *College enrollment statistics [2024]: Total + by demographic.* Education Data Initiative. Retrieved November 29, 2024, from https://educationdata.org/college-enrollment-statistics

2. Fryer, R. G., & Levitt, S. D. (2004). Understanding the Black-white test score gap in the first two years of school. *Review of Economics and Statistics, 86*(2), 447–464.

3. Darling-Hammond, L., & Bransford, J. (Eds.). (2007). *Preparing teachers for a changing world: What teachers should learn and be able to do.* Wiley.

4. Murray, J. (2021, August 5). *Busting the belief gap via regular student assessment.* Fordham Institute. Retrieved November 29, 2024, from https://fordhaminstitute.org/national/commentary/busting -belief-gap-regular-student-assessment

5. Crenshaw, K. W., Ocen, P., & Nanda, J. (2015). *Black girls matter: Pushed out, overpoliced and underprotected.* Columbia Law School. https:// scholarship.law.columbia.edu/faculty_scholarship/3227

6. Carter Andrews, D. J., Brown, T., Castro, E., & Id-Deen, E. (2019). The impossibility of being "perfect and white": Black girls' racialized and gendered schooling experiences. *American Educational Research Journal, 56*(6), 2531–2572. https://doi.org/10.3102/0002831219849392

7. Mims, L. C., & Williams, J. L. (2020). "They told me what I was before I could tell them what I was": Black girls' ethnic-racial identity development within multiple worlds. *Journal of Adolescent Research, 35*(6), 754–779. https://doi.org/10.1177/0743558420913483

8. Devine, P., Forscher, P., Austin, A., & Cox, W. (2012). Long-term reduction in implicit race bias: A prejudice habit-breaking intervention. *Journal of Experimental Social Psychology, 48,* 1267–1278. https://doi .org/10.1016/j.jesp.2012.06.003

PART 2

Build Compassionate and Supportive Connections

Once we have taken the time to reflect on our beliefs and biases, the next essential step is to build genuine, compassionate, and supportive relationships with our students. **Part 2: Build Compassionate and Supportive Connections** focuses on creating a classroom and learning space culture grounded in trust, empathy, and inclusion. The aim here is to not only forge meaningful connections with Black girls but also cultivate an environment where each student feels safe, valued, and understood. This section encourages you to move from reflection to action, using practical tools and strategies that will help you transform your interactions and your classroom dynamics.

Chapter 3: "Practice Two—Plant the SEAD" introduces the idea of social, emotional, and academic development (SEAD). The practice of "planting the SEAD" focuses on creating an inclusive space where every student, especially Black girls, can thrive socially, emotionally, and academically. You will learn strategies that promote emotional intelligence, resilience, and academic growth while reinforcing a sense of belonging. The goal of this chapter is to ensure that each student feels affirmed and supported in a learning environment that encourages their full development—an environment where they are encouraged to bring their authentic selves into the classroom each day.

Chapter 4: "Practice Three—Listen With Compassion" builds on the ideas of fostering a supportive classroom environment through the art of compassionate listening—an essential skill for educators who seek to understand Black girls as whole individuals. This practice goes beyond simply hearing students' words and jumping to solve their problems; it's about deeply listening with the intention of understanding their unique experiences, backgrounds, challenges, and dreams. Through suggested approaches, you'll be encouraged to take a genuine interest in each student's story, allowing you to connect with them on a deeper level. Compassionate listening fosters empathy, strengthens trust, and ultimately allows Black girls to feel seen and respected for who they are, not just for what they achieve.

As you work through this section, the focus will be on building the kind of connections that create lasting change in your classroom. You'll be equipped with practical strategies to nurture empathy, respect, and inclusion, all of which are vital to ensuring Black girls feel truly supported. This part of the journey is about more than just teaching; it's about creating a community within your classroom that honors each student's individuality and fosters a sense of belonging. The compassionate, supportive connections you build here will lay the groundwork for meaningful, transformative relationships that not only improve academic outcomes but also empower your students to achieve their fullest potential.

CHAPTER 3

Practice Two—Plant the SEAD

"Black girls from an early age understand what's happening to them and aren't afraid to define it as sexism and racism."[1]

— Marketa Burnett

IMAGINE THIS

You walk into Ms. Williams's eighth-grade social studies classroom that looks perfect on the surface—desks neatly aligned in rows, students diligently following instructions, and the teacher's voice guiding them through a lesson. It's the kind of classroom that administrators love to see—orderly, focused, and calm. But if you look closer, you'll notice the tension simmering beneath the silence.

Take Lyric, for example, sitting in the second row. She raises her hand occasionally but hesitates before speaking, carefully choosing her words to avoid being labeled as "too loud" or "too aggressive." Last week, during a group project, a peer interrupted her mid-sentence, saying, "We get it, Lyric," with a dismissive tone. It wasn't the first time. She wonders if it's because her voice carries more weight as a Black girl or if she's imagining it.

In the back corner, Jada stares at her notebook, scribbling answers without making eye contact. She remembers how, during a recent class discussion, a male student quickly dismissed her suggestion with "That's not important right now," while others nodded. Ms. Williams didn't catch it, but Jada felt it—a subtle reminder that her voice was seen as secondary.

Brianna, seated near the door, excels in all of her classes but rarely speaks up, feeling that her success goes unnoticed unless it fits within the narrow expectations placed on her. When the class discusses historical figures, Brianna wonders why people who look like her—Black women—are rarely mentioned. The other day, a guest speaker praised the class for their engagement but only called on male students, reinforcing her sense of invisibility.

The teacher, Ms. Williams, is doing her best—walking around, checking work, and offering encouragement—but she can feel something is off. She notices how Lyric hesitates, how Jada seems distant, and how Brianna shrinks into her seat. Despite her efforts to maintain control and ensure academic progress, she senses a disconnection she can't quite name. While every student appears engaged, many are performing for approval rather than learning with joy and confidence.

This classroom scene highlights the critical importance of SEAD in addressing both the visible and invisible dynamics within learning spaces, especially those rooted in subtle gender and racial biases that can stifle student voices and potential.

SEAD IS THE SEED

Before I even thought about this book, I was thinking about SEAD. Before I realized how some learning experiences exclude our Black girls, I thought about SEAD. How many times have we heard the adage that as educators, we are planting *seeds* for the future? First, the play on words is perfect for what it means to create better learning experiences for Black girls.

When we think of a *seed*, we imagine its potential waiting to be unlocked with the right conditions—nutrients, water, sunlight, and care. Similarly, social, emotional, and academic development (SEAD) represents a holistic approach to education that nurtures not just students' academic progress but also their emotional and social well-being. Just as a seed cannot thrive in barren soil, learners need environments that cultivate their full potential. SEAD moves beyond traditional academic metrics by recognizing that emotional resilience, social competence, and cognitive growth are interconnected. When these elements are in balance, students become empowered to succeed both in school and in life.

SEAD: A WHOLE CHILD APPROACH TO STUDENT SUCCESS

The concept of social, emotional, and academic development (SEAD) builds on the foundational work of social and emotional learning (SEL), a movement that gained momentum in the 1990s to address the growing concern over education's narrow focus on academic achievement alone. SEL, championed by organizations like the Collaborative for Academic, Social, and Emotional Learning (CASEL), introduced critical competencies like self-awareness, self-management, social awareness, relationship-building, and responsible decision-making.[2] These skills were designed to promote a well-rounded educational approach, emphasizing emotional intelligence and interpersonal skills alongside academic success.

As SEL grew in prominence, educators and policymakers recognized the need to expand its scope, particularly for diverse and historically marginalized student populations. This evolution led to SEAD, which integrates academic rigor with social and emotional development, recognizing that these elements are inseparable in fostering holistic student success. Unlike SEL's primary focus on individual competencies, SEAD emphasizes the interconnectedness of emotional well-being, social skills, and academic achievement, ensuring students like Lyric, Jada, and Brianna don't just survive the system but thrive within it. Its emergence reflects a deeper understanding that to truly prepare students for success, educational systems must address all facets of a learner's experience, especially in communities where systemic inequities create significant barriers to achievement.[3]

Since the onset of the global pandemic, a myriad of inequities within education have come to light, with some gaps being newly exposed and others significantly widened. The pandemic revealed the critical need for holistic student support, underscoring the urgency of addressing not just academic needs but also social and emotional well-being. In response, the Centers for Disease Control and Prevention (CDC) developed the Whole School, Whole Community, Whole Child (WSCC) model. This comprehensive framework prioritizes the various factors influencing students' health and well-being, including social-emotional climate as a key component. The inclusion of this element in the WSCC model is more than appropriate—it is essential. The model reinforces that positive student outcomes require intentional community and school-based support for the holistic development of learners.

SEAD'S ROLE IN SUPPORTING BLACK GIRLS IN MIDDLE SCHOOL

As we've seen in earlier chapters, the middle school years are a pivotal period for Black girls, marked by both developmental opportunities and significant challenges. Black girls often navigate complex environments where their identities are simultaneously racialized and gendered, facing biases that can impact both their academic engagement and personal growth. You'll recall examples like Lyric's constant self-monitoring, Jada's quiet withdrawal, and Brianna's silent pursuit of excellence, each reflecting a broader trend where compliance and academic performance often come at the expense of authenticity and self-expression.

Despite the remarkable resilience Black girls display, this dual burden of racial and gender biases can result in classrooms that prioritize their outward behavior and academic results over their holistic well-being. The traditional systems in place often fail to affirm their identities or create spaces where they feel valued, which can lead to disengagement and feelings of marginalization. These experiences, as discussed earlier, emphasize the necessity of rethinking how we approach education for Black girls in middle school.

Fortunately, SEAD doesn't just focus on making students "feel good"—it represents an approach that centers the whole child. By addressing the cultural, emotional, and intellectual identities of Black girls, SEAD creates classrooms where students are not only seen and heard but are empowered to rise to their fullest potential. When social-emotional development is thoughtfully woven into academics, the results are profound: enhanced resilience, stronger academic achievement, and, most critically, a deeper sense of belonging.[4]

Belonging, especially for Black girls who may feel underrepresented or overlooked, is more than a buzzword. It's foundational. Feeling like they belong can be the difference between simply getting by and truly thriving. Belonging gives students the courage to show up as their authentic selves, participate fully, and engage deeply in their learning. When Black girls see themselves reflected in the curriculum, in their teachers' belief in their potential, and in the overall culture of their schools, their motivation and engagement flourish.

Take, for example, Mr. Johnson's eighth-grade classroom, where SEAD principles are fully integrated into both instruction and classroom culture. During a unit on historical figures, Mr. Johnson intentionally includes narratives of Black women who have shaped history, such as Fannie Lou Hamer, Claudette Colvin, and Ida B. Wells. Beyond simply teaching these stories, he facilitates discussions that allow students to draw connections between these figures' resilience and their own experiences. In one activity, students are encouraged to share personal stories of overcoming challenges, fostering a space where their voices and lived experiences are validated. Lyric, who once hesitated to speak up, now confidently shares how she navigated self-doubt during a science fair project, inspired by Fannie Lou Hamer's unwavering determination. Jada, who was previously withdrawn, begins to engage in group work, finding strength in knowing her unique perspective is valued. Brianna, who excelled quietly, now mentors her peers, recognizing that leadership is not only about performance but also about community support.

In this SEAD-embedded environment, students experience learning as more than just acquiring knowledge—they see it as a reflection of who they are and who they can become. This not only strengthens their academic outcomes but also deepens their sense of connection and purpose in the classroom.

PAUSE FOR REFLECTION

Have you witnessed a student demonstrating behavior like Lyric, Jada, or Brianna? Based on what you have learned, what do you think they were communicating through their behavior? How might cultivating a stronger sense of belonging for your students impact their motivation and engagement in your classroom or learning space?

CULTURALLY RESPONSIVE SEAD

As we prepare to look at some of the strategies and approaches that you can implement, it is absolutely a must that I make a very important point. Consider it a warning label: SEAD isn't a one-size-fits-all solution. To be effective, it must be culturally responsive, meaning that teaching practices, curriculum, and school environments are designed with a deep understanding of students' cultural backgrounds. To achieve this, scholars like James A. Banks, Geneva Gay, Gloria Ladson-Billings, and Villegas and Lucas have developed influential models of culturally responsive teaching that emphasize integrating cultural diversity into instructional practices, promoting equity, and creating inclusive learning environments. Their work and the studies of others in the field highlight the importance of educators recognizing and honoring the diverse cultural identities of their students, using this understanding to shape teaching methods and content that not only reflect students' lived experiences but also affirm and empower their unique identities. Dena Simmons puts it perfectly: SEL (social-emotional learning) without cultural competence risks becoming "white supremacy with a hug."[5] Ouch, right? But it's true. If we're not careful, any kind of social-emotional development can reinforce the very systems of oppression we're trying to dismantle. In BIPOC (Black, Indigenous, and People of Color) communities, SEL is often pushed as a behavioral control mechanism—teaching kids to "comply" rather than helping them grow. This is the scene that was described at the beginning of this chapter with Lyric, Jada, and Brianna. When students like Lyric feel the need to tone down their voices, Jada withdraws to avoid dismissal, and Brianna remains unseen despite her brilliance, it becomes clear: the classroom may be structured, but it isn't necessarily inclusive. See the problem?

Meanwhile, in predominantly white schools, SEL tends to focus on prepping students for college and careers, often ignoring the cultural richness of BIPOC students.[6] Two things can be true: yes, college and career preparation are important, *and* we can intentionally include experiences that affirm students' identities, address systemic inequities, and create spaces where all students feel seen and valued. Otherwise, we risk reducing education to a tool of conformity rather than a catalyst for meaningful growth.

This gap in how SEL/SEAD is applied highlights the need for educators to approach it with an antiracist lens, ensuring that social-emotional practices do more than manage behavior or prescribe a college or career survey—they must actively dismantle inequities. Scholars like Jagers, Rivas-Drake, and Borowski remind us that SEL should be a tool for justice, not control.[7] When SEL/SEAD is implemented without acknowledging systemic racism and cultural dynamics, it risks becoming another tool that reinforces existing hierarchies, often silencing or marginalizing Black girls and other BIPOC students. An antiracist lens challenges educators to go beyond surface-level strategies and dig deeper into how race, identity, and power influence students' experiences. It calls for a shift from a one-size-fits-all approach to one that recognizes and values the unique cultural strengths each student brings, intentionally creating spaces where every child feels seen, heard, and valued. In short, SEAD without this critical perspective can inadvertently uphold the very biases it aims to counter.

Here's the thing: SEAD isn't just about emotions, social skills, or "fixing" Black students. It's about disrupting an educational system that has historically upheld racial hierarchies through curricula, policies, and practices, such as standardized testing that disproportionately disadvantages students of color, curricula that predominantly feature Eurocentric perspectives while neglecting the histories and contributions of marginalized communities, and disciplinary policies like zero-tolerance that disproportionately impact Black students.[8][9][10] If we're serious about equity, we need to actively dismantle these structures—and SEAD can be a powerful tool for doing just that. When educators bring cultural competence and an antiracist lens to SEAD, they're not just teaching social skills; they're building equitable spaces where Black girls and other marginalized students can thrive academically, socially, and emotionally. SEAD, done right, can challenge these inequities and create learning environments where Black girls are uplifted, not policed.

But let's be clear: SEAD alone isn't enough to combat systemic racism. As Simmons emphasizes, no amount of emotional intelligence can shield BIPOC students from the realities of systemic oppression.[11] SEAD must go beyond feel-good strategies to confront the cultural, racial, and social contexts shaping students' lives. Only then can we create educational spaces that intentionally support Black girls.

Returning to Ms. Williams's classroom, imagine a SEAD-driven approach where every student feels seen and valued. Lyric's voice is heard without judgment. Jada's curiosity is encouraged. Brianna's achievements are celebrated in ways that reflect her unique strengths. This is the promise of SEAD: classrooms where Black girls—and all students—are uplifted, not policed, and where they can rise to their fullest potential.

THE EDUCATORS' ROLE IN ADVANCING SEAD FOR BLACK MIDDLE SCHOOL GIRLS

Now that we have laid a firm foundation, I'm sure you are eager to do this work, and you are probably wondering, *Okay, but how do I plant this SEAD you so passionately speak about, Melody?* I'll walk you through a few key themes revealed in research studies that show SEAD's impact. From fostering a sense of belonging to building resilience and integrating culturally responsive teaching, these strategies have empowered Black girls to rise academically and socially. By the end of this section, you'll see why

SEAD isn't just a "nice-to-have." It's a must—a tool for equity, transformation, and true educational justice.

Social, emotional, and academic development (SEAD) is a transformative approach, but its success depends on how it is implemented by different educators. Each role—whether teacher, administrator, counselor, or community partner—contributes uniquely to cultivating a supportive environment for Black middle school girls. The following section explores research-backed strategies tailored to each role, offering actionable, easy-to-implement practices that can be adapted to various educational contexts.

CLASSROOM TEACHERS: EMBEDDED SEAD INTO CLASSROOM CULTURE

Classroom teachers are the heartbeat of a space where Black middle school girls can develop emotional intelligence (self- and social awareness) and build academic resilience. Research by Hammond highlights how culturally responsive teaching strengthens these abilities, empowering students to manage their emotions and navigate academic challenges.[12]

Research further emphasizes that SEL interventions improve emotional regulation and foster positive peer interactions, contributing to a more inclusive classroom culture.[13] By integrating SEAD strategies into daily practice, educators can empower students, affirm their identities, and foster resilience.

Below is a summary of impactful strategies that teachers can implement in their classrooms:

- **Culturally Responsive Representation:** Use materials that reflect students' identities to foster belonging and engagement.

- **Questioning Strategies and Metacognition:** Use techniques that encourage students to think critically about their own thinking processes.

- **Intentional Relationship Building:** Build trust through regular, meaningful interactions.

- **Teaching Emotional Regulation and Resilience:** Incorporate resilience-building activities to support self-management.

- **Centering Student Voice:** Empower students by integrating their perspectives into classroom decisions and activities.

STRATEGY	DESCRIPTION	IMPACT	EXAMPLE
Culturally Responsive Representation	Use instructional materials that reflect Black girls' and Black women identities, contributions, and experiences.	Builds self-esteem, fosters a sense of belonging, and increases engagement, motivation, and academic success.	*Feature modern-day Black women scientists in a science lesson.*
Questioning Strategies and Metacognition	Use techniques that encourage students to think critically about their own thinking processes and engage in higher-order questioning.	Promotes deeper understanding, self-reflection, and independent problem-solving skills.	*Use open-ended questions like, "What strategies did you use to solve this problem, and why?" to encourage metacognition.*
Intentional Relationship-Building	Build trust through genuine, consistent connections with Black girls and prioritize listening to their experiences.	Encourages emotional safety, fosters a supportive learning environment, and increases willingness to seek help.	*Schedule weekly one-on-one check-ins to discuss academic progress and personal goals.*
Teaching Emotional Regulation and Resilience	Embed mindfulness and resilience-building activities into daily routines.	Enhances self-management skills, improves focus, and supports perseverance in overcoming academic challenges.	*Begin class with an exercise such as box-breathing or guided affirmations.*
Centering Student Voice	Empower students by integrating their perspectives into classroom decisions and activities, ensuring their voices shape their learning experiences.	Builds confidence, fosters ownership of learning, and creates a more engaging and inclusive classroom environment.	*Facilitate classroom meetings where students provide input and propose classroom norms.*

Here is an example of how I supported my students' emotional regulation and resilience.

USING THE ONE WORD PROJECT TO BUILD EMOTIONAL REGULATION AND RESILIENCE

The One Word Project is a simple yet powerful way to help students focus on self-regulation and resilience by encouraging them to commit to a single guiding principle. Inspired by the ideas presented in the One Word Project,[14] I implemented the following steps in my classroom:

STEPS TO IMPLEMENT
THE ONE WORD PROJECT

1. **Introduce the Concept With an Article**

   - As a class, we read a short article discussing how New Year's resolutions often fail because they are too broad or unsustainable. The article emphasizes how focusing on one word can lead to greater success and meaningful change.

   - We discussed the data together, and students shared examples of resolutions they had struggled to maintain.

2. **Choose a Word**

   - I provided students with a list of potential guiding words (e.g., *resilience, focus, kindness, courage, balance*).

   - Each student chose a word that resonated with them—something they wanted to embody or commit to in their daily lives at school.

3. **Create a One-Pager**

   - Students designed one-pagers centered on their chosen word. These included
     o the word written in bold letters;
     o a brief explanation of why they chose it; and
     o drawings, symbols, or colors that reflected its meaning.
     o The one-pagers were anonymous, so no one knew whose word belonged to whom.

4. **Display in the Classroom**

   - I posted the one-pagers all around the classroom, creating a vibrant and inspiring visual display.

   - During a class discussion, I explained that if they ever felt overwhelmed, discouraged, or distracted, they could look at their one word to refocus and find strength.

5. **Maintain the Focus Throughout the Year**

   - Periodically, I would revisit the display and ask students to share (voluntarily) how their word was guiding them.

   - I integrated reminders of their words into lessons, class goals, and individual check-ins.

SCHOOL ADMINISTRATORS: LEADING SEAD SCHOOLWIDE

School administrators hold the power to embed SEAD into the very fabric of the school's culture. Khalifa et al. highlight how equity-driven leadership dismantles systemic barriers and promotes inclusivity, which is crucial for Black middle school girls.[15]

When administrators prioritize social-emotional professional development, it strengthens teacher capacity and student outcomes.[16] Administrators can lead systemic changes that promote inclusivity, amplify student voices, and support teachers in meeting the unique needs of Black girls. Strategies such as providing SEAD-centered professional development, promoting restorative practices, and ensuring representation in leadership and curriculum can have a transformative impact.

Here are some key strategies administrators can use:

- **Cultivate an Inclusive School Culture:** Foster an environment where Black girls feel valued and supported.

- **Promote Restorative Discipline Practices:** Address behavioral issues with restorative justice methods rather than punitive measures.

- **Elevate Student Voices:** Create platforms for Black girls to contribute to school decision-making processes.

- **Support Mental Health:** Provide culturally competent counseling and safe spaces for Black girls to process emotions.

- **SEAD-Centered Professional Development:** Train educators to integrate social-emotional and academic development practices across all disciplines.

STRATEGY	DESCRIPTION	IMPACT	EXAMPLE
Cultivate an Inclusive School Culture	Build a school environment that celebrates diversity and equity by embedding these values into daily practices, policies, and school expectations.	Enhances feelings of belonging, self-worth, and motivation; reduces feelings of isolation or marginalization.	*School leadership routinely review and audit student leadership roles (student council, peer mentors, ambassadors) to ensure equitable access and diverse representation, adjusting selection processes to address bias.*

(Continued)

(Continued)

STRATEGY	DESCRIPTION	IMPACT	EXAMPLE
Promote Restorative Discipline Practices	Shift from punitive discipline to restorative approaches that focus on repairing harm and building relationships.	Reduces suspensions and expulsions for Black girls, builds trust with adults, and encourages positive behavior change.	*Use restorative justice circles to address conflicts, giving students a platform to voice concerns and work toward resolutions together.*
Elevate Black Girls' Voices	Provide opportunities for Black girls to share their experiences and influence school decisions that affect them.	Increases student agency and leadership; strengthens the connection between students and the school environment.	*Ensure Black girls are represented and encouraged to participate in student leadership opportunities.*
Support Mental Health and Wellness	Offer culturally responsive mental health services and create safe spaces where Black girls can process emotions and experiences.	Improves emotional resilience and coping skills, leading to better focus and academic performance.	*Establish an affinity group for Black girls to connect, share, and access support from knowledgeable staff.*
SEAD-Centered Professional Development	Train educators to incorporate social, emotional, and academic development practices into teaching and schoolwide initiatives.	Builds teacher capacity to support the holistic development of Black girls and ensures consistency in equitable practices.	*Conduct professional learning workshops on implementing SEAD strategies and addressing implicit bias in the classroom.*

SCHOOL COUNSELORS AND SUPPORT STAFF

Counselors and support staff are often the first line of support in helping Black middle school girls build resilience and develop coping skills. School counselors who partner with educators to address students' needs can create a stronger, more meaningful impact.[17] Research indicates that when school counselors collaborate, programs and services are more effectively customized and systematically implemented to address the unique needs of every student.[18] Counselors help Black girls develop essential life skills, fostering both emotional well-being and academic success.

Some effective approaches include

- **Advocating for Inclusive Policies:** Collaborate on schoolwide policies that eliminate systemic barriers.

- **Establishing Mentorship Programs:** Connect students with role models to inspire and guide their development.

- **Strength-Based Counseling:** Use a strength-based approach during individual sessions to help Black girls identify and leverage their unique talents and abilities.

- **Family Partnerships:** Work with families to create collaborative plans that support Black girls' academic and social-emotional growth at home and school.

- **Restorative Check-In Places:** Create safe spaces for Black girls to talk about and receive support for issues they face.

STRATEGY	DESCRIPTION	IMPACT	EXAMPLE
Advocacy for Inclusive Policies	Partner with school leaders to advocate for policies and practices that eliminate barriers and foster a more equitable learning environment.	Reduces inequities, improves access to resources, and ensures Black girls' voices are heard in school decisions.	*Collaborate with school leadership on revising the school's dress code or discipline policies to remove biased language and practices that disproportionately affect Black girls.*
Mentorship Programs	Establish mentorship initiatives that pair Black girls with role models who share similar cultural backgrounds and can offer guidance and inspiration.	Provides representation, fosters aspiration, and builds strong support networks.	*Launch a program connecting Black girls with local professionals or high school students for regular mentoring sessions.*
Strength-Based Counseling	Use a strength-based approach during individual sessions to help Black girls identify and leverage their unique talents and abilities.	Encourages a positive self-concept, resilience, and academic and personal growth.	*During one-on-one sessions, guide students to create "personal achievement plans" focused on their strengths and future goals.*
Family Partnerships	Work with families to create collaborative plans that support Black girls' academic and social-emotional growth at home and school.	Strengthens trust, aligns home and school strategies, and builds a strong support system for students.	*Host workshops like "Navigating Middle School Together," offering tips for parents to support their child's success and well-being.*
Restorative Check-In Spaces	Create safe spaces where Black girls can debrief challenging experiences, receive emotional support, and reenter the classroom ready to learn.	Reduces stress, enhances emotional regulation, and fosters a sense of safety and trust in school counselors.	*Design a "wellness room" where students can reflect, journal, and connect with counselors during moments of stress or conflict.*

COMMUNITY EDUCATORS AND PARTNERS: EXTENDING SEAD BEYOND THE CLASSROOM

Community educators and organizations have a unique opportunity to extend SEAD beyond the school walls, ensuring its impact reaches every corner of a student's life. A report commissioned by the Wallace Foundation emphasizes that partnerships between schools and out-of-school-time programs significantly enhance social-emotional learning by fostering supportive environments and consistent SEL instruction, leading to improved student outcomes.[19] After-school and out-of-school-time programs provide Black girls with safe, supportive spaces where they can develop academically, socially, and emotionally.

Here are some approaches that community educators and partners can take:

- **Community Service and Leadership Projects**: Provide opportunities for Black girls to engage in community service projects that allow them to lead and make a positive impact in their local community.

- **Mindfulness and Stress-Relief Activities**: Integrate mindfulness practices, meditation, and stress-relief activities to help Black girls manage emotions and stress in a safe space.

- **Restorative Practices**: Implement restorative circles where girls can discuss conflicts, repair harm, and strengthen relationships in a non-punitive way.

STRATEGY	DESCRIPTION	IMPACT	EXAMPLE
Community Service and Leadership Projects	Provide opportunities for Black girls to engage in community service projects that allow them to lead and make a positive impact in their local community.	Builds leadership skills, encourages a sense of responsibility, and strengthens social awareness and community bonds.	*Facilitate service projects like organizing a neighborhood cleanup or volunteering at a local food bank, empowering students to take leadership roles.*

STRATEGY	DESCRIPTION	IMPACT	EXAMPLE
Mindfulness and Stress-Relief Activities	Integrate mindfulness practices, meditation, and stress-relief activities to help Black girls manage emotions and stress in a safe space.	Promotes emotional regulation, stress reduction, and greater self-awareness, leading to improved emotional resilience.	*Lead group mindfulness exercises such as breathing techniques or guided meditations after school to promote calmness and focus.*
Restorative Practices	Implement restorative circles where girls can discuss conflicts, repair harm, and strengthen relationships in a non-punitive way.	Teaches accountability, conflict resolution, and communication skills, fostering a supportive environment for growth.	*Set up restorative justice circles after conflicts in the program, allowing Black girls to express their feelings, listen to others, and repair relationships.*

The practice of planting SEAD may look different depending on the role of the educator, but the outcome remains the same: Black middle school girls who are emotionally resilient, academically motivated, and empowered to thrive in the face of challenges. Whether you're a classroom teacher fostering emotional intelligence, an administrator leading systemic change, a counselor providing trauma-informed support, or a community partner extending SEAD beyond the school walls, your role is vital. Together, these efforts create a learning environment where SEAD is not just an option—it's a necessity for equity and transformation. And as you take on this journey, remember that the real benefits lie in how SEAD supports Black girls. It cultivates a classroom culture that is inclusive, empathetic, and supportive, empowering all students to thrive in a diverse, ever-changing world. By nurturing emotional intelligence, self-esteem, supportive relationships, coping skills, and authentic expression, you're breaking down barriers and fostering a transformative educational experience that empowers Black girls to overcome stereotypes and confidently navigate their path forward.

In the Middle

Plant the SEAD

In this section, take a moment to reflect on the information and strategies shared throughout the chapter. Consider how the approaches outlined earlier can help create a more inclusive learning environment where Black girls feel supported, respected, and valued. Reflect on which of these approaches you can begin to implement in your own setting. Think about how choosing one strategy might help foster emotional intelligence, resilience, and academic success. This reflection is an opportunity for you to consider practical steps that will allow all students to bring their authentic selves and feel a true sense of belonging.

REFLECTION TASK

Take a moment to reflect on the following questions. Choose one or all three to think deeply about. Consider how each question relates to your work and how you can use these reflections to improve the support you provide for Black girls in your learning environment. There are no right or wrong answers—just an opportunity to explore your thoughts and identify areas for growth.

1. **Which SEAD approach could make the biggest difference?** Think about the SEAD strategies shared earlier. Which one do you feel could have the greatest positive impact on creating a supportive environment for Black girls in your learning space? Is there another strategy you've used or thought about that could work well too?

   _____

   _____

   _____

2. **How do you create space for students to grow emotionally?** Reflect on how you currently help students with their emotional and social development. How can you bring in or build on SEAD practices to better support Black girls in your environment?

   _____

   _____

   _____

3. **Where can you grow in supporting SEAD?** Think about an area where you'd like to do better in supporting Black girls' emotional and social development. How can one of the SEAD strategies—or something new you try—help make that improvement?

   _____

   _____

   _____

Vision-Casting to Plant the SEAD

A Vignette of Empowering Black Girls in the Classroom

I had the privilege of leading a vision-casting session with a group of 25 educators and school leaders, each deeply invested in creating an educational experience that would serve our students well. At first, we were uncertain how to integrate all our diverse ideas into a cohesive vision, knowing that each of us had unique passions and perspectives on what students needed. Yet, there was a shared understanding that our ultimate goal was to empower students to become their best selves, both academically and personally.

Our conversation began with two guiding questions:

- *What do we want our students to embody when they leave our school?*

- *Who do we want our students to be? What skills do we want them to have?*

While the conversation naturally turned to academic achievement, it quickly became clear that the real focus wasn't just on specific content areas like math or science. As a passionate science educator, I didn't bring up the formulas or facts I teach. We all realized that it wasn't the content that mattered most, but the deeper skills students developed through learning. Skills such as persistence, compassion, and effective communication emerged as key priorities—skills that transcend the classroom and prepare students for life beyond school.

It was in that moment that I realized the importance of social, emotional, and academic development (SEAD) in shaping the whole child. For our students to truly thrive, we needed to teach not just math or reading, but also the skills that help them navigate the world with confidence and awareness. SEAD is about cultivating a space where students feel empowered to grow emotionally and socially, alongside their academic success.

This became especially clear when we discussed the unique challenges faced by Black girls in our classrooms. Their experiences are often shaped by systemic barriers, implicit bias, and a lack of representation in curricula. These obstacles are compounded by the stereotypes and microaggressions that they face daily, both in and outside the classroom. Yet, as educators committed to equity and empowerment, we knew that SEAD could serve as a powerful counterforce to these challenges.

We envisioned a school where Black girls weren't just surviving but thriving—where their identities were not just acknowledged but celebrated. This wasn't just about improving their academic performance; it was about helping them develop the resilience and emotional intelligence to overcome adversity. It was about fostering an environment where they could grow into confident, compassionate leaders who could transform their communities and the world around them.

In this vision, SEAD became the cornerstone of an educational experience that recognized Black girls as whole people—minds, bodies, and emotions. It wasn't

(Continued)

(Continued)

enough to wish for their success; we had to actively create an environment that nurtured their self-confidence, affirmed their identities, and provided them with the tools to succeed. We couldn't just focus on their academic growth; we had to ensure they had the emotional and social tools to navigate a world that often marginalizes them.

As educators, we knew we had to go beyond good intentions. SEAD required us to design learning experiences and policies that were culturally responsive and inclusive. We needed to provide training for all adults who interact with students, ensuring they were equipped with the strategies to best support Black girls. From curriculum to classroom climate, SEAD would infuse every aspect of the school day with an understanding of who our Black girls are and what they need to flourish.

This work wasn't easy, but it was necessary. And the payoff would be immeasurable. By planting the seeds of SEAD, we would not only transform the educational experience for Black girls but also contribute to a more just and equitable society. Through intentional, responsive, and inclusive teaching, we could empower Black girls to thrive—academically, socially, and emotionally—and help them become resilient leaders who could transform the world.

This vision for Black girls is the future of education we must build. A future where SEAD is more than a framework; it is a lived experience that empowers every student to reach their fullest potential.

NOTES

1. Mims, L., Burnett, M., Martin, R., Leath, S., & Harris-Thomas, B. (2023). "Black Girl Magic is everything:" Recommendations for cultivating supportive spaces for Black girls. *Theory Into Practice, 63*(1), 68–76. https://doi.org/10.1080/00405841.2023.2287721

2. CASEL. (2023, March 3). *What is the CASEL framework?* Retrieved from https://casel.org/fundamentals-of-sel/what-is-the-casel-framework/

3. Darling-Hammond, L., Flook, L., Cook-Harvey, C., Barron, B., & Osher, D. (2019). Implications for educational practice of the science of learning and development. *Applied Developmental Science, 24*(2), 97–140. https://doi.org/10.1080/10888691.2018.1537791

4. Aspen Institute. (2018). *Seizing the moment: Integrating social, emotional, and academic development.* Retrieved from https://www.aspeninstitute.org/wp-content/uploads/2018/04/ESSA-IntegratingSocialEmotionalAcademicDevelopment.pdf

5. Simmons, D. (2019). You can't be emotionally intelligent without being culturally responsive: Why family and consumer sciences must employ both to meet the needs of our nation. *Journal of Family and Consumer Sciences, 111*(2), 7–16.

6. Simmons, D. (2019). Why we can't afford whitewashed social-emotional learning. *ASCD Education Update,* 61(4).

7. Jagers, R. J., Rivas-Drake, D., & Borowski, T. (2018). *Equity and social and emotional learning: A cultural analysis.* Retrieved from https://measuringsel.casel.org/wp-content/uploads/2018/11/Frameworks-Equity.pdf

8. Kim, K. H., & Zabelina, D. (2015). Cultural bias in assessment: Can creativity in assessment help? *International Journal of Critical Pedagogy, 6*(2), 129–147. https://uscaseps.org/wp-content/uploads/2020/07/standardized-testing.pdf

9. DaCunha, J. C. M. (2016). Disrupting Eurocentric education through a social justice curriculum. *International Development, Community and Environment (IDCE),* 25. https://commons.clarku.edu/idce_masters_papers/25

10. Ford, S. (2021). Learning while Black: How "zero tolerance" policies disproportionately affect Black students. *University of Florida Journal of Law & Public Policy, 32*(1), Article 2. https://scholarship.law.ufl.edu/jlpp/vol32/iss1/2

11. Simmons, D. N. (2019). How to be an antiracist educator. *ASCD Education Update,* 61(10). https://www.ascd.org/el/articles/how-to-be-an-antiracist-educator

12. Hammond, Z. (2014). *Culturally responsive teaching and the brain: Promoting authentic engagement and rigor among culturally and linguistically diverse students.* Corwin.

13. Rivers, S., & Salovey, P. (2011). Emotional intelligence: Implications for personal, social, academic, and workplace success. *Social and Personality Psychology Compass, 5,* 88–103. https://doi.org/10.1111/j.1751-9004.2010.00334.x

14. One Word Project. (2020, December 28). Retrieved from https://mrcssharesease.wordpress.com/one-word-project/

15. Khalifa, M. A., Gooden, M. A., & Davis, J. E. (2016). Culturally responsive school leadership. *Review of Educational Research, 86*(4), 1272–1311. https://doi.org/10.3102/0034654316630383

16. Darling-Hammond, L., Wechsler, M. E., Levin, S., Leung-Gagné, M., & Tozer, S. (2022). *Developing effective principals: What kind of learning matters?* [Report]. Learning Policy Institute. https://doi.org/10.54300/641.201

17. Hunter, T. (2020). *Guiding the socio-emotional Learning of African American middle school girls through the perspective of school counselors* [Thesis, Concordia University, St. Paul, MN]. Digital Commons. https://digitalcommons.csp.edu/cup_commons_grad_edd/469

18. Barna, J., & Brott, P. (2012). Elementary school counselors' motivation to support student academic achievement through identified standards. *Journal of School Counseling*, 10(8), 1–36.

19. Jones, S. M., Brush, K. E., Wettje, S., Ramirez, T., Poddar, A., Kannarr, A., Barnes, S. P., Hooper, A., Brion-Meisels, G., & Chng, E. (2022, November). *Navigating SEL from the inside out: Looking inside and across 18 leading SEL programs: A practical resource for schools and OST providers—Middle and high school focus*. Harvard Graduate School of Education. https://doi.org/10.59656/yd-os7616.001

CHAPTER 4

Practice Three—Listen With Compassion

> "Trusting Black girls to voice what they desire in a
> free and safe space is an act toward liberation."[1]
>
> — Maya White

In my first year of teaching, everyone told me that the first year would be my survival year. I'm sure my colleagues were trying to ensure that my first year would not end with me running as far away from the classroom as possible. My mentors and supporters constantly reminded me that year one is the year to learn what *not* to do in the years ahead. I constantly tried to get through each class period with my students, who expected me to know everything. I would often say that my students are consistent at being persistent. They never accepted "I don't know" as an answer from me—their teacher.

While managing the challenges of teaching, I began to see that this first year wasn't just about survival; it was about discovery. I was learning not only how to teach but also about the lives of my students—their triumphs, their frustrations, and the disparities they faced. My role as their teacher required more than delivering science lessons; it required understanding who they were beyond the classroom.

To help paint a picture of my students' experiences, allow me to share some data: the Black community in the city where I taught represents approximately 16.1% of the city's population,[2] and, as reported by the 2020 U.S. Census, the Black poverty rate is over three times the national average of 11.4% and surpasses the city's overall poverty level of 22.5%.[3] At the heart of the Black community lies the middle school where I served, teaching a population of more than 80% Black and LatinX students. These statistics underscored what I observed daily—my students' experiences outside of school directly impacted their engagement, motivation, and achievement in the classroom.

Understanding these realities forced me to approach my teaching differently. I couldn't be an effective teacher without first getting to know my students on a deeper level. This realization led me to lean into *Practice Three—Listen With Compassion*.

Compassionate listening became a transformative practice in my classroom. It is the act of actively and empathetically engaging with another person's story, striving to understand their emotions, needs, and experiences without judgment. In education, this approach is particularly powerful. Hammond emphasizes that compassionate listening is essential for marginalized students, as it validates their lived experiences while empowering them to see themselves as valued and capable learners.[4]

One conversation with Drika completely reshaped how I approached student discussions and highlighted the importance of creating affirming spaces for Black girls in learning environments. Drika often refused to participate in class discussions, and when I asked her privately why she hesitated, she replied, "I don't want to hear what other people have to say." At first, her comment seemed dismissive, but I decided to ask more questions to understand her perspective.

I gently asked, "Why do you feel that way?" She shrugged at first but eventually admitted, "Because nobody wants to hear what I have to say." Her words broke my heart and illuminated a deeper issue. I followed up, asking, "Do you feel like there's space for your ideas in class?" and "What do you wish was different about the way we talk and share?" Her responses revealed how excluded she often felt, both by her peers and the classroom dynamics.

Drika's experience made me realize that I wasn't doing enough to create a space where Black girls felt seen and valued. It led me to completely rethink how I facilitated discussions. I introduced science-specific accountable talk strategies, intentionally teaching students how to listen actively, respond thoughtfully, and engage in ways that respected everyone's contributions.

I also made it a priority to regularly affirming Drika's ideas during small group activities and celebrating her insights in whole class discussions. The transformation was powerful. But I wouldn't have done that without first listening with compassion to what Drika said.

This practice isn't just a tool; it's a mindset. And while it may sound simple, it demands intention, persistence, and vulnerability.

FROM THEORY TO PRACTICE

I realized early on that becoming a compassionate listener required me to go beyond the surface. I had to put aside my assumptions, listen not just with my ears but with my heart, and embrace the perspectives of my students. By doing this, I began to build trust and open the door to more meaningful connections.

They often sought me out to share their experiences and ask questions, both about academics and life. My Black girl students would open up about topics like navigating their academic journeys, caring for their hair, building self-esteem, and finding their way in spaces as young Black girls. Others confided in me about peer relationships and managing responsibilities at home. These moments weren't just about giving advice—they were about truly listening and being present for them.

One of the most memorable examples involved a group of girls who would linger after class to talk. They shared their challenges and dreams, and I could see how my presence as a Black woman in STEM provided them with representation they didn't often see. Years later, one of those girls reached out to tell me that those after-class conversations inspired her to believe in her potential. Today, as a college student pursuing engineering, she still credits those moments as the turning point that gave her the confidence to chase her dreams.

These moments shaped my understanding of what it means to be an educator. As I moved into my second year of teaching, I grounded my work in a vision and mission: to provide culturally relevant and equitable science learning experiences that help my students become positive contributors to their community.

This mission drove me to reimagine my classroom as a space where students felt seen, heard, and valued. For example, I introduced projects that connected science to real-world issues they cared about, such as environmental justice and health disparities in their neighborhoods. I once had a student create a presentation on lead contamination in drinking water and how it disproportionately affects communities like hers. This project not only deepened her understanding of chemistry but also empowered her to advocate for change in her own community. I had another student research the composition of lip gloss and decided to make her own, natural lip gloss.

Achieving this vision, however, required compassionate listening as a foundation. I came to see that listening deeply and intentionally to my students wasn't just an effective practice—it was an essential step toward creating the kind of classroom culture they needed to thrive.

HONORING THE VOICES OF BLACK GIRLS

This practice is especially critical for Black girls. Historically, schools have imposed expectations on Black girls about how to behave, dress, and learn, yet the system has often failed to listen to their voices with empathy and compassion. The report *Listening to Black Women and Girls: Lived Experiences of Adultification Bias* by the Georgetown Law Center on Poverty and Inequality highlights that educators have not always done a great job of hearing and valuing Black girls' perspectives. Instead, their experiences are often overlooked, and their voices dismissed.[5] This lack of attentive listening has left many Black girls feeling misunderstood and unsupported in educational spaces.

As an educator, I saw firsthand that what Black girls need most isn't more instructions about how to conform—it's someone who will truly hear and value their stories. One day, a student stayed behind after class and shared her frustration about being labeled "too loud" or "too bossy" by her peers and teachers. "I'm not the only one who has stuff to say, but I always get called out," she said. Her words stayed with me because they echoed what the Georgetown report reveals: Black girls frequently experience environments where their thoughts and feelings are minimized or misinterpreted.

One of the key findings of the Georgetown study emphasizes the importance of communication as a tool to improve interactions between authorities and Black girls. Participants in the study highlighted that better communication—grounded in listening with compassion—could lead to more accurate interpretations of students' intentions and emotions. This improved understanding between teachers and students can help avoid inappropriate disciplinary responses that often stem from mis-interpretation or bias. Listening with compassion, therefore, becomes not just an act of empathy but also a practical strategy for fostering trust and mutual respect.

This conversation also reflected what Monique Morris highlights in her work: Black girls are often punished for their confidence and self-expression, leading to feelings of alienation.[6] Listening to this student without judgment allowed me to affirm her right to speak up and to help her channel her strengths in a way that empowered her rather than silenced her.

By creating opportunities to truly listen to Black girls and prac-ticing open, compassionate communication, educators can foster a sense of belonging and affirmation. The simple act of listening—free of judgment and bias—can be transformative, offering Black girls the validation they need to thrive. Schools must commit to valuing the voices of Black girls, ensuring that they are not just heard but also respected and supported.

While this chapter focuses on the importance of listening to Black girls, Chapter 7 will go into more detail about the concept of adultification bias and how it impacts Black girls in educa-tional spaces. For now, it's crucial to recognize that meaningful change begins with listening to Black girls, practicing compas-sionate communication, and making space for their stories to be heard.

Compassionate listening builds a classroom environment of trust and safety, and students can have more ownership of their learning in a safe environment. They are more willing to take academic risks in pursuit of achievement. As Martha Caldwell highlights, when students' need to belong is fulfilled through compassionate listening and supportive relationships, they feel safer, which fosters trust and reduces fear-driven behaviors, allowing them to take academic risks and engage more deeply in their learning.[7] When I took the time and intentionally lis-tened to my students more, I saw increased engagement and decreased behavioral interruptions. And, yes, that also led to increased student achievement. I used this same practice of compassionate listening with all my students but made sure to be intentional with my Black girl students. This has also shown up in my daily life as an administrator. I can recall a specific time when I had to give a student a consequence for her behavior, and as I walked her back to class, she said, "Thank you, Ms. Hawkins." Of course, I had to ask her why she was thanking me when I gave her a behavior consequence she did not want. She responded, "Thank you for listening to me. I just needed someone to listen."

The next phase of my mission was to model compassionate listening so that my students, teachers, and community support system can demonstrate this as a regular part of our daily interactions and make a tri-fold impact. There is a powerful *impact* made when compassionate listening occurs. In true educator fashion, IMPACT is more than just a word. It is also an acronym that I have developed for practicing compassionate listening. Aligning the IMPACT acronym to what is necessary for Black girls' safety and vulnerability in educational settings produces the following insights, and this is how you can do it, also:

> **I - Intentional:** Be *intentional* when Black girls speak and expect to deepen your understanding of their statements. Think: *I want to listen to understand, not just to listen.* By doing so, you validate their experiences and perspectives, which can foster a stronger and more positive relationship. Avoid invalidating their feelings or dismissing their words, as this can create distance and harm.

> **M - Mindful:** Be *mindful* of your body language. Think: *I must be mindful of my body language: What are my hands doing? Where are my eyes? What is my body communicating?* If I am sitting with a student, I turn my body toward them and loosely mimic their posture, close my laptop, push my phone away, and sometimes I even announce that I am doing these things to ensure I am entirely focused on them. This is important for Black girls because they often feel ignored or belittled in academic settings. By being mindful of body language, we show them they are valued and heard, which can positively impact their confidence and academic performance.

> **P - Pause:** Be ready to *pause*. Think: *I have to pause my thoughts, my own biases, my perceptions, and my eagerness to go into fix-it mode.* We are educators and advocates who love teaching, talking, having the answers, and problem-solving. But when someone shares their truth, their knowledge, we have to remember that it's not about what we think; it's about them. It's about how they feel, what they know, what they perceive, and what they need. We always need to pause and listen without judgment. What does this do for Black girls? Pausing and listening without judgment creates a space where Black girls can express themselves freely and feel heard. It also acknowledges their experiences and validates their perspectives.

> **A - Authentic:** Be *authentic*. We always want to remember that our authenticity validates the speaker's feelings. Overall, demonstrating *authenticity* while listening

involves being fully present, engaged, and honest in your interactions with the other person. In this case, authenticity refers to who I am in the conversation. I may not understand the topic fully or have all the answers, but being genuine in my responses makes the interaction meaningful and impactful. It allows for honest and authentic connections rather than just surface-level exchanges. I do not need to change who I am and be someone else to connect with the person speaking. This is important for Black girls because it empowers them to embrace their authentic selves without feeling like they must conform to societal norms or expectations. It also allows them to form genuine connections with others who accept and appreciate them for who they are.

Perhaps my favorite part of this acronym is "C" for community.

C - Community: Build a *community*. Being compassionate builds community between the listener and the speaker; for whatever reason, the speaker chose you to be their listener. Maybe it was a default decision because no one else was around, perhaps it was a strongly encouraged decision (as it sometimes is when I have spoken with a student in my office), or maybe they sought you out, but the point is that they are sharing their story with you. This may be the only opportunity to build that community of trust and safety with the speaker, so we must remember that "community" exists as soon as they speak to you. Feeling like they have a community is a necessary experience for Black girls in school. Creating a community where Black girls feel safe and heard positively *impacts* their academic outcomes and well-being. As a listener, it is essential to actively cultivate such a space and be receptive to their experiences.

T - Time: Be clear about *time*. Think: I have to be clear about my availability and time to devote to being a listener. Even with the best intentions, if we cut the speaker short right as they prepare to open up, that can be a detriment to the relationship. I can damage the community that was beginning to form. So, being transparent about how much time I have at the beginning is a must. Being clear about the time I can devote to being a listener directly counteracts the feelings of not being heard, often experienced by Black girls. This is particularly important when trust needs to be established between individuals. It can also help to personalize the interaction and create a more meaningful exchange within the community.

A caring listener can completely change a student's academic and social-emotional path as a teacher, administrator, mentor, or support system. It's something that I practice daily, and I practice it with the assumption that others are watching how I navigate conversations as a listener and with the hope that I can be an ever-developing demonstration of compassionate listening. By modeling these skills consistently, teachers, administrators, and mentors can create an environment where everyone is inspired to practice active and empathetic listening. This can lead to better student engagement and improved academic and social outcomes for all involved.

COMPASSIONATE LISTENING PROMPTS TO BUILD TRUST AND SAFETY

To create a classroom environment where Black girls feel safe to express themselves and take academic risks, educators can use open-ended questions that demonstrate care, curiosity, and an intent to understand. Here are some questions to guide compassionate listening conversations:

1. **"What's been on your mind lately, and how can I support you?"**

   This question invites students to share freely and signals that their concerns are valued.

2. **"Can you tell me more about how you're feeling right now?"**

   This validates the student's emotions and opens the door for deeper understanding.

3. **"What do you think is the biggest challenge you're facing in class (or school), and what would help make it better?"**

   By centering their perspective, you show a commitment to working with them to address barriers.

4. **"What's something you wish teachers or adults understood about you?"**

   This empowers students to voice their unique needs and perspectives.

5. **"What's one thing that makes you feel proud of yourself, and how can we celebrate that?"**

   This shifts the focus to their strengths and builds confidence.

6. "When things get tough, what do you think helps you bounce back?"

   This question encourages reflection on resilience and self-management strategies.

By using these prompts, educators can create opportunities for students to feel heard, understood, and supported. This intentional practice not only nurtures trust but also inspires students to take ownership of their learning and engage more deeply in the classroom.

THE IMPACT OF COMPASSIONATE LISTENING

Now that you understand what goes into compassionate listening, I'd like to show you what it can look like in practice. I can't think of a better illustration than the story of how Ms. Mitchell listened with compassion and, as a result, potentially saved the life of one of her students.

The first thing you must know about Ms. Mitchell is that she is a fantastic teacher! Not just because the state test scores say so or because her students think so, but because her passion for teaching is evident in everything she does. Ms. Mitchell goes above and beyond to create engaging lessons that cater to the individual needs of her students, ensuring that they not only grasp the material but also develop a love for learning. Ms. Mitchell has dedicated her skillset of English instruction to a high-needs community for six years. She enjoys watching her students push past negative stereotypes and is always there to support their journey, even after leaving her class. Not surprisingly, Ms. Mitchell has constantly developed meaningful relationships with her students and often has private one-on-one with individual students while others are working during class. Not just to talk about their academic work but also to check in on their developmental work—for instance, how they manage their classwork, friendships, responsibilities at home, or extracurriculars.

One day during these check-ins, as she spoke with her Black girl student, China, Ms. Mitchell noticed something different. China had always been a bright, cheerful presence in her classroom, but now her eyes seemed dimmed, and her enthusiasm for learning had waned. This was the first clue that something was amiss, and Ms. Mitchell's intuition told her to dig deeper.

With the ease of a trusted confidante, she gently inquired about China's well-being, not just academically but emotionally. China hesitated at first, but as she saw the genuine concern in Ms. Mitchell's eyes, she began to open up. She revealed that she had been struggling with depression for a while and believed that nothing she tried was working. Tears welled in her eyes as she shared the overwhelming feelings that had crept into her life.

Ms. Mitchell's compassionate listening provided the lifeline China desperately needed. Rather than dismissing her struggles or providing easy solutions, Ms. Mitchell sat with China, listened without judgment, and assured her she was not alone in this journey. She encouraged China to seek help from her school counselor. Ms. Mitchell not only alerted the school counselor, but also followed up with the counselor even after transferring the information. Over time, China began her path to recovery, and it was clear that Ms. Mitchell's support played a pivotal role in her healing. Ms. Mitchell continued to be there for China, ensuring her academic work was manageable and that she felt safe and supported in the classroom. Their bond deepened as a teacher and student and as allies in navigating the complexities of life.

A significant point to mention here is that when Ms. Mitchell shared the conversation with China's counselor and administrators, they were stunned that China had been carrying such feelings. They never saw this side of China. They never would have guessed that China was struggling in this way. What sets Ms. Mitchell apart is her extraordinary ability to create a safe space where students feel comfortable sharing their deepest fears and anxieties. She is keenly aware of the importance of genuinely listening, and when she asks, "Tell me how you're feeling right now," it isn't a mere formality but an invitation for her students to open up without fear of judgment. The students know very well that by talking to Ms. Mitchell, they are talking to an adult who cares and will do something about their concerns.

China's story is a compelling testament to the profound impact of compassionate listening, particularly in supporting the well-being of Black girls in educational settings. Ms. Mitchell's steadfast commitment to her students extends far beyond textbooks and lesson plans, embodying deep empathy and genuine care that she demonstrates in bold and intentional ways. She doesn't just tell her students she cares about them socially, emotionally, and academically—she shows it through the way she thoughtfully plans her lessons, manages her classroom with fairness and respect, and holds them accountable in both their work ethic and social interactions. By fostering this trust and creating a sanctuary for her students, Ms. Mitchell instills in them the belief that they are valued, their struggles are acknowledged, and they are not alone in their challenges. For students like China, this intentional approach makes it clear that Ms. Mitchell's care is authentic, which is why, when it came time to have a hard conversation, China knew she could trust her. While there were other teachers like Ms. Mitchell in this school, China only had the fortune of having one of them. What if China did not have access to Ms. Mitchell at all?

In a society where stereotypes and systemic barriers have long burdened Black girls and women, Ms. Mitchell's ability to prioritize emotional and mental well-being alongside academic success highlights the essential role educators play in creating safe, inclusive environments where students feel seen, valued, and empowered to thrive.

Throughout history, Black girls and women have been burdened with the expectation of unwavering strength and resilience. They have been expected to endure silently, persevere without showing vulnerability, and carry the weight of their struggles and the injustices heaped upon their communities. These enduring stereotypes have perpetuated the idea that Black girls and women are invincible, are immune to pain, and need not express their vulnerabilities. This toxic narrative leaves Black girls in a precarious position. It tells them they must be firm and not ask for help or seek solace in moments of despair. Such stereotypes, ingrained in societal perception, make it challenging for Black girls to open up about their struggles. They feel pressured to hide their pain, believing that revealing their vulnerabilities is a sign of weakness or an acknowledgment of stereotypes they have fought hard to overcome.

This perception has been deeply ingrained over centuries, from the days of slavery when Black women's pain was often dismissed or minimized, to the present, when societal views still often expect Black women to withstand suffering without complaint. Research shows that these harmful stereotypes continue to shape societal views of Black women, making it difficult for them to express pain without facing the repercussions of being labeled as "weak" or "overreacting." As a result, Black girls may internalize these narratives, something known as Superwoman Schema, suppressing their pain and emotional distress to conform to an image of unyielding strength. Yet, Ms. Mitchell's classroom broke through this cycle of silence and isolation. Ms. Mitchell's compassionate listening offered them an alternative narrative that said expressing their emotions and vulnerabilities was not just acceptable but essential. In her classroom, Black girls could release the burden of "invincibility" and feel safe to be vulnerable, knowing that their emotions were heard and valued.

Ms. Mitchell may not have realized this, but she perfectly demonstrated the IMPACT necessary to engage in compassionate listening. And it was a safety net for her students. China's story is a powerful reminder of the transformative impact of educators who provide such safe spaces. By breaking down these entrenched stereotypes, educators can empower Black girls to embrace their authenticity, acknowledge their struggles, and seek the support they need. It's not just about learning academic lessons; it's about dismantling societal constructs that have silenced Black girls for generations.

THE POWER OF COMPASSIONATE LISTENING

The IMPACT acronym guides the practice of listening with compassion: being intentional, being mindful, pausing to listen without judgment, being authentic, and creating a sense of community. Understanding the importance of time and setting clear expectations makes the interaction meaningful and allows trust and safety to flourish.

As I continually model these skills for my students, teachers, administrators, mentees, mentors, and support systems, I envision a future where compassionate listening is a cornerstone of our educational approach. By fostering environments where everyone is inspired to practice active and empathetic listening, we can enhance student engagement, academic success, and social-emotional well-being for all involved. Reinforcing compassion and empathy are powerful tools for dismantling the barriers that Black girls face in educational settings. As we embark on the journey of transformation, we are reminded that, in students' hearts, the true impact of compassionate listening extends far beyond the classroom, reaching the realms of life itself.

In the Middle

Listen With Compassion

In this section, take a moment to reflect on the information and examples shared for listening with compassion throughout the chapter. Think about how actively listening will contribute to a learning environment where every Black girl feels supported. This reflection is an opportunity for you to consider practical steps that will allow all students to bring their authentic selves and feel a true sense of belonging.

REFLECTION TASK

Take a moment to reflect on the strategies outlined in this chapter for listening with compassion. Reflect on the following questions:

1. **How can you be more intentional in your listening, ensuring that you truly understand and validate the perspectives of Black girls in your classroom?** Think about how you can deepen your understanding of Black girls' perspectives and ensure their experiences are validated.

   _____

   _____

   _____

2. **In what ways can you be more mindful of your body language and actions to communicate that you are fully engaged and creating a space where Black girls feel heard and valued?** Consider how you can use these cues to create a space where Black girls feel heard and valued.

   _____

   _____

   _____

3. **What are one or two go-to questions you can prepare to ask that will help foster open communication and show your commitment to listening with compassion?**

   _____

   _____

   _____

NOTES

1. White, M. (2020). *"SHE WILL TELL ME THE TRUTH": Listening to Black girls co-organizing liberatory spaces* (Thesis, Georgia State University). https://doi.org/10.57709/18617975

2. U.S. Census Bureau. (2024, June 27). *U.S. Census Bureau QuickFacts: Knoxville city, Tennessee*. Retrieved December 9, 2024, from https://www.census.gov/quickfacts/fact/table/knoxvillecitytennessee/POP060210

3. To end gun violence, leaders say, Knoxville must alleviate stifling Black poverty. (2022, September 28). *Knoxville News Sentinel*. Retrieved from https://www.knoxnews.com

4. Hammond, Z. (2014). *Culturally responsive teaching and the brain: Promoting authentic engagement and rigor among culturally and linguistically diverse students*. Corwin.

5. Blake, J. J., & Epstein, R. (2019, May 14). *Listening to Black women and girls: Lived experiences of adultification bias*. Georgetown Law Center on Poverty and Inequality.

6. Morris, M. W. (2016). *Pushout: The criminalization of Black girls in schools*. The New Press.

7. Caldwell, M. (2017). *How to listen with compassion in the classroom: When we teach compassionate listening to students, we foster belonging, inclusion, and learning in the classroom*. https://www.researchgate.net/publication/317612389_How_to_Listen_with_Compassion_in_the_Classroom_When_we_teach_compassionate_listening_to_students_we_foster_belonging_inclusion_and_learning_in_the_classroom

Advocate for Her Development and Childhood

In this pivotal third section, you will explore how to empower Black girls and advocate for their growth and well-being in the classroom and beyond. **Part 3, *Advocate* for Her Development and Childhood**, focuses on the critical role educators play in supporting the unique needs of Black girls by actively standing up for their rights, fostering their self-esteem, and preserving their girlhood. As we transition from building compassionate relationships to taking action, this section will provide you with practical techniques to not only understand the challenges Black girls face but also advocate for their development with intention and purpose. By empowering Black girls to feel seen, valued, and heard, you will become a champion for their holistic growth and success.

Chapter 5: "Practice Four—Encourage Positive Self-Talk" will guide you through strategies to help Black girls build self-confidence and resiliency. The emphasis here is on supporting each girl to articulate her worth, voice her opinions with authority, and believe in her potential. This practice provides actionable tools for fostering positive self-talk, allowing students to reframe negative internal narratives and take pride in their achievements. Through empowering Black girls to see themselves as leaders, educators can spark their self-empowerment and resilience, preparing them to succeed both inside and outside the classroom.

Chapter 6: "Practice Five—Advocate for Their Girlhood" shifts the focus to the impact of societal pressures that adultify Black girls, expecting them to "know better" and navigate adult challenges at a young age. This chapter will provide you with strategies to protect the sanctity of their childhood by advocating for an environment where their girlhood is not only respected but celebrated. You will learn how to create a classroom space that shields Black girls from these unfair societal expectations, while also providing them the freedom to express themselves without the weight of premature adultification.

Chapter 7: "Partnering With Families and Communities" broadens the conversation to include the larger systems and networks that impact Black girls' lives. This chapter will provide strategies for you to build a strong support system for Black girls by collaborating with families, community members, and mentors. By driving systemic change, you will ensure that Black girls are not only supported in their immediate educational environment but also empowered to thrive in their broader community.

This section is not just about advocacy; it's about being a proactive, informed, and dedicated ally for Black girls, ensuring they grow in environments that respect their rights, celebrate their identities, and equip them for leadership. The reflective questions presented here will allow you to begin thinking deeply about how to champion Black girls' rights, enhance their self-assurance, and promote a culture of advocacy that extends far beyond the classroom, creating lasting, systemic change in the communities they call home.

CHAPTER 5

Practice Four—
Encourage
Positive Self-Talk

---

*"Deal with yourself as an individual worthy of
respect and make everyone else deal with you the same way."*

— Nikki Giovanni

Deficit narratives and stereotypes about Black girls have not only impacted their views of themselves (referenced in Chapter 2) but have also created a barrier to Black girls' ability to find positive language to identify themselves. This lack of positive language creates a lack of confidence—confidence that is needed to approach complex academic tasks and take academic risks. By fostering an environment that promotes positive self-talk, teachers can empower Black girls to develop a strong sense of self-worth and belief in their abilities. This, in turn, can help them overcome challenges and excel academically, breaking down the barriers that have hindered their progress in the past.

Positive self-talk is a concept that perfectly falls under the social and emotional learning umbrella. However, it is so critically necessary for our Black girls that it deserves its own section. It is more than just a skill or a strategy in many ways. This is the "super tool" that Black girls need to keep themselves empowered in the face of adversity. Black girls often face unique challenges and negative messages about their worth and abilities, and positive self-talk can help them combat these harmful narratives and build confidence in themselves.

WHAT IS SELF-TALK?

Self-talk is the inner dialogue we all have running in our minds. It's that voice in your head that comments on your actions, interprets situations, and shapes how you view yourself and the world. Sometimes it's loud and clear: "You nailed that presentation!" Other times, it whispers doubts: "You'll never figure this out." Self-talk influences our emotions, decision-making, and confidence in profound ways.

Self-talk operates in several forms. Self-talk significantly influences our mindset and behavior. Positive self-talk is uplifting and focuses on strengths, while negative self-talk is critical and exaggerates weaknesses. Motivational self-talk fosters effort and perseverance, whereas demotivational self-talk reduces enthusiasm by emphasizing barriers. Context-dependent self-talk is practical and tailored to specific tasks, while global self-talk involves broad statements that shape identity. Each type of self-talk can impact emotions, motivation, and performance.

Here's a breakdown of the types and characteristics of self-talk:

TYPE OF SELF-TALK	DESCRIPTION	EXAMPLES
Positive Self-Talk	Uplifting and constructive, focuses on strengths and possibilities.	"I've prepared for this, and I'll do my best."
Negative Self-Talk	Critical and discouraging, often exaggerates weaknesses or failures.	"I'm going to mess this up again. I always fail."
Motivational Self-Talk	Encourages effort, perseverance, and a can-do attitude.	"Keep going—you're almost there!"
Demotivational Self-Talk	Diminishes effort or enthusiasm by focusing on barriers and setbacks.	"Why bother? It's not like this will work out."
Context-Dependent Self-Talk	Tailored to specific situations or tasks, often immediate and practical.	"I need to slow down and read the question carefully."
Global Self-Talk	Broad, general statements about oneself, often shaping identity.	"I'm just not good at anything."

This mental chatter can be automatic or deliberate, global or context-specific, and, most importantly, positive or negative.[1] When positive, self-talk can encourage perseverance and confidence during challenges. The intentional practice of reframing those inner conversations to focus on strengths, solutions, and growth helps us to avoid being overly critical of our mistakes. In doing this, we use self-talk to lift ourselves up, stay motivated, and move forward with a constructive mindset. On the flip side, negative self-talk can diminish motivation and create self-doubt, making even small tasks feel insurmountable.

For Black girls in middle school, self-talk can be shaped by both internal and external factors. As we have discussed in earlier chapters, at this critical developmental stage, many Black girls face harmful societal stereotypes, deficit narratives, and implicit biases in school environments that label them as "too loud," "aggressive," or "unmotivated." These messages, whether subtle or overt, can easily seep into their inner dialogue, reinforcing feelings of inadequacy or difference. If left unchecked, negative self-talk can lead to disengagement, lower self-esteem, and self-doubt. For instance, when Black girls encounter disproportionate disciplinary actions for behaviors that are overlooked in their peers, they may internalize messages like *"I must be the problem"* or *"No one understands me."* These moments make teaching them to reframe their inner dialogue an essential intervention.

POSITIVE SELF-TALK IN LEARNING SPACES

Positive self-talk isn't just an act of encouragement—it's equipping Black girls with a life skill to resist internalizing biases and rewrite their own narratives of success and empowerment. Encouraging affirming messages like *"I am smart and capable"* or *"I have a voice that deserves to be heard"* helps them navigate spaces that might otherwise feel isolating or invalidating.

The way Black girls speak to themselves profoundly impacts their self-perception, approach to challenges, and ability to bounce back from setbacks. Positive self-talk can be a transformative tool for Black girls in many ways:

- **Counters Negative Narratives:** Black girls often face stereotypes such as being "bossy" or "difficult." Positive self-talk helps them resist these labels, replacing them with affirmations of their leadership and individuality.

- **Improves Self-Esteem:** Positive self-talk reinforces a belief in one's abilities, boosting confidence that may be undermined by biases in the classroom.

- **Encourages Resilience:** Positive self-talk shifts the focus from problems to solutions, helping students stay motivated even when encountering racial or gender-based challenges.

- **Enhances Academic Performance:** When Black girls believe in their abilities, they are more likely to engage fully in learning, ask questions, and take academic risks.

Encouraging positive self-talk is a powerful and essential practice for educators to foster in their students, particularly for empowering Black girls. There will be times when Black girls must fill themselves with resilience and confidence as they navigate challenging situations. These situations may include facing discrimination, stereotypes, or unequal treatment. Black girls need to remember their worth and embrace their unique identities, knowing that they have the strength to overcome any obstacles that come their way.

Equipping Black girls with tools to cope with adversity not only enhances their ability to thrive but also helps them overcome barriers they may encounter. By modeling positive self-talk, educators create an affirming environment where students learn how to approach challenges with self-compassion and confidence. It's not just about telling students to "think positively"— it's about demonstrating what that looks and feels like in real time, providing them with tangible examples they can emulate.

When I share stories about Black girls' struggles in school that I have witnessed, people sometimes develop a narrative suggesting that this little Black girl might be from a household that doesn't value education or lacks positive adult influences. However, this is not necessarily true and is no more likely to be the case for a Black girl than for any other student. While there are certainly situations where a lack of support at home could contribute to a student's challenges, it is important to avoid making assumptions. Because race and ethnicity do not inform socioeconomic status (meaning just because a person is Black does not mean they are living in poverty or uneducated homes), even Black girls from stable home environments are impacted by societal stereotypes and low expectations that create a negative impact on their self-esteem and motivation to succeed academically.[2]

While the premise of this book rests on the experiences of Black girls in middle school, it is also important to illuminate how their early interactions with societal biases, systemic inequities, and cultural expectations shape their sense of self, academic achievement, and overall well-being, laying the foundation for their future resilience and empowerment. After all, research shows that educators can begin developing biases against Black girls as early as preschool.

Let's look at an example of how societal stereotypes and biases can impact even the most supported Black girls. And this little girl, you know. Let's talk about my daughter, Miah.

MIAH'S STORY

Coming from a home with highly supportive parents—both of whom hold multiple college degrees and work in education—you might think she would be shielded from adversity. Yet even she felt the weight of societal stereotypes and the challenges they bring.

Miah has always been my little empathetic, loving, people-centered sweet girl. She loves wholeheartedly and always looks for ways to support others around her. In 2020 Miah was so excited to start kindergarten, even though it was the middle of the pandemic. She had spent all her young years watching her big sister, Madison, go to school, so Miah was ready to start her learning journey. It was time for the school year, and she was ready. All her materials were packed in her backpack (including extra masks and hand sanitizer). She jumped head-first into her classes and was ready to fly. Kindergarten was fun and filled with joy for her. But in first grade, that flame started to dim a bit. I noticed that she was not as excited to go to school as she once was.

As a teacher, I know these can be the unintended yet predictable emotions about school that any student may develop. However, I could tell something had changed with Miah. Something was different. Her father and I dug deep into conversation with Miah and asked question after question about school one day. And then she finally told me, "It feels weird being the only one who looks like me in my classes. Everyone else looks alike, but I don't. My hair is different—I want long pigtails. My skin is different, and I sometimes talk different. It's just different. Everyone else is the same. But I'm so different." Those were the words of my 6.5-year-old. And, despite growing up in a supportive household, and her dad and I preparing her for the world's diversity, Miah faced challenges in her school environment due to her unique appearance and ethnic background.

Despite our efforts to instill confidence and self-acceptance in her, she still struggled with feeling like an outsider among her peers. These external influences challenged her confidence and self-perception, impacting her emotional well-being at a young age. It reminded us that no matter how much we prepare our children, they will still face challenges navigating their unique identities in a homogenous environment. However, we remain committed to supporting and helping her embrace her differences and recognize them as strengths. We knew we had to find ways to empower her and help her navigate these obstacles while embracing her individuality.

I was preparing to talk with her teacher to make her aware of the changes we noticed with Miah but guess what—I didn't have to. Why not? Because this teacher saw very clearly that Miah needed something more in her learning environment. This teacher intentionally worked to build Miah's confidence, not just as a student but as a young Black girl in a class of mostly white peers. I knew something had changed when I saw Miah's joy for school come back. She was excited again, hopeful, optimistic, saying things like, "Yep, I can do this because I'm smart. Mrs. Lane tells me all the time." I saw my then 7-year-old daughter, Miah, move from being a shy, bright, compassionate, nurturing little Black girl to one more confident about her place in this big world.

Miah's teacher had poured so much positive language into Miah that Miah was finally doing it for herself. Even with Miah's father and I always telling her positive things about herself, it was the thoughts of her teacher that began to influence her perception of herself. Mrs. Lane's consistent use of positive language reinforced the self-confidence we were building in Miah and provided her with a different perspective on herself. As a result, Miah's self-perception started to align more closely with the empowering messages she received from her teacher, transforming her outlook on what she has to offer this world. Although I have seen the power of educators in shaping the mindsets and self-esteem of their students, it was a completely different experience to witness this impact firsthand with my own child. It reaffirmed for me how critical it is for educators to intentionally use their words and actions to uplift, inspire, and empower, especially for Black girls who often face a world that undermines their potential. In Miah's case, her teacher's belief in her abilities became a powerful counterbalance to any doubts that might have crept into her mind.

Positive self-talk empowers Black girls to embrace their unique identities and equips them with the resilience needed to navigate societal challenges. It helps Black girls overcome obstacles and thrive in all aspects of life by fostering a strong sense of self-worth and affirming their capabilities. Her teacher knew how to use positive self-talk to help Miah navigate in a classroom where she was one of few Black girl honor students—something that Miah frequently commented about. Miah's teacher understood the importance of representation and inclusivity in the classroom. By acknowledging Miah's achievements and highlighting her strengths, the teacher created an environment where Miah felt seen and valued. This not only boosted Miah's confidence but also encouraged her to excel academically, proving that positive self-talk can profoundly impact a student's success. And, no, the teacher was not Black herself, showing yet another piece of evidence that all teachers must know and understand how to support Black girls in the classroom. This teacher's ability to empower Miah and create a supportive environment for her demonstrates the importance of educators being culturally competent and aware of the unique challenges faced by Black girls. By acknowledging and addressing these challenges, teachers can help foster confidence, resilience, and success in their students, regardless of their racial background.

Self-talk, as a concept, can take many forms. It may be positive or negative, motivational or demotivational, global or context-specific, and either automatic or deliberate.[3] Positive self-talk has been identified as a critical factor in helping individuals persevere through stressful and challenging situations. By engaging in motivational and constructive self-dialogue, students can build the mental resilience needed to navigate adversity and maintain their focus on achieving goals. For Black girls, who often encounter unique social and academic challenges, fostering positive self-talk serves as a vital tool to help them counteract negative stereotypes, nurture their self-worth, and thrive despite external pressures.

Remember, consistent and intentional efforts to foster positive self-talk can help Black girls build resilience, confidence, and a strong sense of self-worth. These strategies can empower them to overcome challenges and excel academically.

LAYLA'S STORY

But what happens if this positive self-talk does not happen? What happens if Black girls never or rarely *intentionally* hear strengths-based language about themselves and therefore never really learn how to use positive self-talk as a tool for empowerment? That is the story that I will tell you about next. Hang on, this will be a journey of emotions for sure.

It was a beautiful sunny afternoon in October when I sat across from a former student. She had been with me since she was an eighth grader in my science class during the strangest year in our educational journeys—fall 2020. Now, she sat across from me at a conference room table as a 10th grader in our high school. In my mind, she will always be the eighth grader who bopped around my classroom, looking at the lab coats and playing with the human body models, looking every bit like the nurse she said she wanted to be. To others in high school, she stood out effortlessly as a girl trying to find her place in the world. With stormy eyes and tousled ebony hair, usually in braids, sometimes in short twists, she navigated with boldness and practicality uncommon in her peers. Her directness draws people in despite her claim of not caring for friendships. A hint of vulnerability occasionally surfaces when she is willing to let her guard down. Beneath her tough exterior, she has a spirit that remains unbroken. In the school's microcosm, she's a contradiction—boldly indifferent yet quietly yearning.

Since I accidentally followed Layla to high school as an administrator, she often sought me out for her dose of encouragement. She knew she was special to me, and I knew I was special to her. I was there with her during the hard moments of a hybrid virtual/in-person eighth-grade school year. In the awkward transition to ninth grade and my transition to an administrator, I was there helping her navigate new teachers, a new school environment, and she was there for me, unbeknownst to her, while I was navigating life as a new administrator. And now, here we sat together at a table in the school building.

We had spoken frequently over the weeks that led to this moment. Usually, the conversations were about how she is trying to focus as a 10th grader and not be involved in drama. Occasionally, I would hear her complaints about how she felt that her teachers didn't care. She did not say that often, so I did not often have to respond to such sentiments. I usually saw her around 10:45 a.m.—at the tail end of second block. So, between her complaints and funny stories about the neighborhood happenings that she frequently kept me aware of, I would throw in a "Tomorrow, be on time for school!" Or "I sure wish I could see you in the early mornings instead of just before lunch!" And even once, I said, "Do I need to start giving you a wake-up call?" to which we both laughed.

But the more I saw her in the weeks leading to this table chat, I began to hear her say more and more with a very matter-of-fact tone that her teachers did not care about her. After experiencing the loss of so many students to gun violence, I have vowed never to take for granted a student's statement of how they feel in their classroom because that classroom may be the only opportunity that they have to feel safe, carefree, not worried about what waits around the corner. So, when I started to hear her saying this with more conviction, I began to pass her reflections to her grade-level administrators and counselor. One time, I even spoke with the teachers whose classes she frequently missed due to her chronic delay to see what work she could do to get caught up because her grades were slipping hard and fast. All of that led to this day, *the table chat.*

It was a normal day for me as completed my normal check-ins and classroom rounds in the building. Amid my movement from hallway to hallway, I ran into some of my 10th-grade students close to this student. They said, "Ms. Hawkins, did you know Layla is going to move to homeschool? Tell her not to! We want her to stay at school with us!" I was shocked because she had not shared that with me, and I had seen her quite a few times. When I finally saw her that day, it was late afternoon, nearing dismissal, and I snagged my opportunity to pull her to the side to see what these rumors were about. She said, "Yea, it's true. My ma got the paperwork. She came up here and talked to everyone, and I'm doing it. I'm going to homeschool." That is when I said, "Let's go chat in the conference room."

I then called in one of her administrators to join the conversation. This is when I learned how much she had been carrying on her shoulders. She shared much about her past, things I did not know. She connected some of the dots I knew about her life as a younger girl, and now her hard exterior began to make even more sense. Layla had experienced the trauma of an inconsistent homelife, having to live in foster care and separated from her siblings, watching countless key family members pass away and all of this happened between the ages of 9 and 13. As she shared, it made even more sense why she loved my science class.

She had begun to find peace and normalcy when she was at school. The school was important for her as a growing Black girl. The school gave her the kid freedom that she deserved. The school gave her something to look forward to and brought her the social interaction that reminded her that she is a kid—innocent—a person who needs to and deserves to be taken care of and treated preciously. School became her sanctuary, a refuge from the chaos and instability. She felt a sense of belonging and stability within my classroom walls. In those precious hours at school, she could temporarily escape the hardships of her reality and simply be a child, free to learn, grow, and dream of a brighter future.

While sitting at the table with her, I made these connections as she shared about her life as a young girl and would weave in and out of experiences that she had in my classroom and the moments that she carried as a treasure. Some of the moments we laughed about. I listened to her intensely, pausing between the laughs, before finally asking, "Layla, what's changed? You seemed so charged up about doing well this school year. I understand that homeschooling is a great option for some. But you enjoy being at school, so what's going on?" And that's when tears started rolling out of these stormy brown eyes down her face. Through the tears and shaky, high-pitched voice, she said, "These teachers don't care about me! They don't ever tell me when I'm doing good. Just when I'm doing bad. They don't care that I feel bad. They just act like *whatever* when I tell them! The last time I felt like a teacher cared about me was you, Ms. Hawkins! In your class! That was the last time!"

She almost yelled those words to me. I felt her frustration and her pain. Whether true or not, this was her reality—that her teachers did not care, so why be at a school, in a class with a teacher who does not care? Do I believe her teachers did not care about her? Absolutely not! I refuse to believe that there were teachers in the school who simply did not care about our students. But do I believe that her teachers may not have known how to or maybe never even thought about how to model the positive self-talk to a Black girl who had been through a lot? Yes, I believe that to be true.

Please do not assume that I am bashing her teachers. It is important to acknowledge that teachers may not always be aware of every student's specific needs and experiences, especially when it comes to addressing issues related to race and trauma. Her teachers may have lacked the necessary training or resources to effectively support her in developing positive self-talk skills. However, this is an example of why it is so crucial for educators to continuously strive for tools and actively seek ways to create a supportive and inclusive learning environment for all students. We, as educators, never really know the impact we are having on a student, so we must treat each encounter as if it is the most important and last encounter that our students might experience with us.

PRACTICAL STRATEGIES FOR ENCOURAGING POSITIVE SELF-TALK

What does it look like to encourage positive talk? Encouraging positive self-talk involves intentionally creating opportunities for students to recognize and build on their strengths while fostering a mindset of self-belief and resilience. This can be achieved by acknowledging and celebrating their accomplishments, highlighting their unique capabilities, and reframing negative thoughts into empowering ones. As an impactful adult in their lives, you can model positive self-talk by sharing affirmations and verbalizing strategies for maintaining a constructive inner dialogue, providing students with a powerful example to emulate. Additionally, offering genuine compliments and consistent encouragement reinforces their confidence and self-esteem.

- **Affirmations and Celebrations**

  Integrate regular affirmations and celebrations into routine interactions. Recognize and celebrate the unique strengths and achievements of Black girls. Create opportunities for them to share their academic, personal, or creative successes. By highlighting their accomplishments, you will foster a sense of pride and self-worth within them.

  - **Give Specific Praise:** Focus on effort, growth, and resilience. For example, say, "I'm really impressed with how much effort you put into that project," rather than just praising the outcome. This reinforces the value of persistence and learning.

  - **Acknowledge Achievements Publicly:** Share individual successes with the class to build confidence and make students feel valued. For example, you might say, "I want to highlight how [Student's Name] worked hard on this assignment and showed great improvement."

  - **Celebrate Small Wins:** Take time to acknowledge even small accomplishments, such as completing a task on time or participating in class. Say things like, "Great job finishing that activity! Your effort really shows."

  - **Create a Recognition Space:** Set up a place in the classroom to celebrate student achievements. This could be a bulletin board with student work, a "student of the month" section, or a digital display to highlight accomplishments.

  - **Involve Families in Recognition:** When students achieve something notable, send a note or email home to celebrate their success. This reinforces the idea that their achievements are recognized and appreciated at school and at home.

  - **Use Culturally Relevant Affirmations:** Include affirmations that resonate with students' cultural backgrounds. For example, celebrate their unique perspectives and experiences, such as saying, "Your perspective in today's discussion really showed your strength and insight." This helps students feel seen and valued for who they are.

- Intentional Modeling

Model positive self-talk yourself! Express optimism and confidence in your abilities and demonstrate how to handle challenges with a growth mindset. By showcasing self-assured behavior and language, you can set an example for Black girls, helping them internalize similar attitudes toward themselves. For example, if you make a mistake while solving a math problem on the board, you might say, *"Oh, I see where I went wrong. That's okay—I can fix this and learn from it."* This approach fosters authenticity, normalizes personal growth, and promotes a sense of empowerment.

  o **Be Authentic:** When you model positive self-talk, you show students that even adults experience self-doubt but can choose to counter it constructively. Share your own challenges and how you overcome them. For example, when struggling with a difficult task, say, "This is tough, but I know I'll get better if I keep practicing."

  o **Normalize Growth:** Reinforce that making mistakes or facing setbacks is a normal part of learning and growing. For example, when something doesn't go as planned, say, "It didn't work out this time, but that's okay. I can learn from this and do better next time." This shows students that learning is a process, not a reflection of their worth or intelligence.

  o **Model Resilience and Empowerment:** For Black girls, seeing an adult navigate biases, setbacks, or challenges with confidence and resilience is incredibly empowering. When something doesn't go as planned, model how you regain focus, use problem-solving skills, and stay determined. For example, "I know this is challenging, but I won't give up because I have the skills to succeed." This helps students understand they too can handle adversity and take control of their self-perception.

- Reframing Negative Thoughts

When Black girls express self-doubt or negative thoughts, encourage them to reframe them positively. Teach them to recognize when they're being too hard on themselves and guide them in transforming those thoughts into affirming statements. For instance, if a student says, "I'm not good at this," help them reframe it as, "I'm still learning, and I can improve with effort." There are some ways that you can walk alongside your student to reframe negative thoughts.

- ○ **Recognize and Validate Their Feelings:** Remind them to acknowledge the negative thought and their emotions without judgment.
- ○ **Challenge the Negative Thoughts:** Ask them if the thought is true and if there's evidence to support it. Consider other ways to view the situation.
- ○ **Replace the Thought With a Positive Thought:** Try to replace the negative thought with a more positive or realistic one.

The narratives of Miah and Layla demonstrate the profound influence educators can have on Black girls' lives. They also emphasize the responsibility of modeling positive self-talk and fostering environments where all students feel valued and supported. Every interaction, every word, and every moment with a student is an opportunity to uplift and inspire, and these opportunities should not be taken lightly.

A teacher or adult in charge of a learning environment can pour positive self-talk at any point in the relationship. A few words can completely change a young Black girl's perception of their current experiences. It does not fix the adversity in the world, but it does offer a safe place for Black girls to go when they need a reminder of who they are—they can turn to the positive library of words they have built about themselves and have seen modeled by the adults in their life.

In the Middle

Encouraging Positive Self-Talk

Encouraging positive self-talk can involve acknowledging and celebrating Black girls' accomplishments, reminding them of their strengths and capabilities, and reframing negative thoughts into positive ones. It can also involve modeling positive self-talk and providing affirmations and compliments.

In the space below, you will use one of these approaches to begin this work.

REFLECTION TASK

Take a moment to reflect on the strategies outlined in this chapter encouraging positive self-talk. Reflect on the following questions:

1. **Affirmations and Celebrations:** How can you purposefully integrate regular affirmations and celebrations into your classroom routines to acknowledge and honor the distinctive strengths and achievements of Black girls? How might you create meaningful opportunities for them to showcase their successes, whether they are academic, personal, or creative, to foster a deep sense of pride and self-worth?

_____

_____

_____

2. **Intentional Modeling:** Make your commitment to demonstrating positive self-talk while you are in the learning environment. For instance, when you make an error, what will you say about yourself? How will you model growth mindset?

_____

_____

_____

3. **Reframing Negative Thoughts:** When you hear one of your Black girl students make a negative comment about themselves, how will you reframe that idea? How will you use this opportunity to give them a positive thought about themselves?

_____

_____

_____

NOTES

1. Reyes, Z. B. (2016). *Self-talk and resilience: Impacts of performance in undergraduates* [Master's thesis, San Francisco State University]. San Francisco State University Digital Repository. Retrieved May 5, 2025, from https://scholarworks.calstate.edu/downloads/ng451k31d

2. Lloyd, R. (2021). *Teacher biases and expectations: Impact on self-esteem, self-efficacy, delinquent behavior among Black grade school students* (Publication No. 607) [Doctoral dissertation, Florida School of Professional Psychology, National Louis University]. Digital Commons. Retrieved from https://digitalcommons.nl.edu/diss/607

3. Reyes (2016).

. . . .

CHAPTER 6

Practice Five— Advocate for Their Girlhood

"Driving change takes a lot of courage, and it takes the willingness to challenge an organization regardless of how big it is."

— Alicia Boler Davis

Meet Madison, my oldest daughter—a bright, determined pre-teen balancing the joys of childhood with the complexities of adolescence. She pours her passion into crafting, crocheting, gymnastics, playing the flute, and dance, while navigating the maze of self-discovery. And, like many Black girls her age, Madison's journey is layered with challenges and triumphs shaped by her identity.

But when Madison noticed the differences in her treatment as a little Black girl, I felt mixed anger, sadness, confusion, and frustration. One story she shared still lingers with me: A classmate took a pencil from her desk—a pencil Madison said she had clearly labeled with her name. When she alerted the teacher, the classmate claimed it as their own. The teacher sided with the other student until Madison, growing agitated, pointed out her name written on the pencil. Only then was she believed.

This incident became a turning point. Madison started noticing similar patterns—moments when her voice or perspective was dismissed by peers or adults. "Why do I have to work so hard just to be believed?" she asked me one evening, her frustration palpable. These moments of feeling unheard or invalidated left deep impressions, chipping away at her confidence and making her question her value in spaces where she should have felt empowered.

As educators, we must ask ourselves: How often do we inadvertently dismiss or undervalue the experiences of Black girls in our classrooms? What would it take to consistently affirm their voices, amplify their strengths, and celebrate their contributions?

I've carried Madison's insights into my work as an educator, knowing that every Black girl like her deserves more than recognition—they deserve advocacy. Teachers have the power to transform classrooms into spaces where Black girls feel valued and capable of shaping their futures.

STAND UP FOR BLACK GIRLS

Madison has always been resilient, quick to shake off frustration and refocus on her goals. But at the end of her fifth-grade school year, something shifted inside her. When I have shared with other Black women the story that you are about to read, I have witnessed their connectedness to Madison's feelings and experiences. I remember one Black woman saying, "Yep, I know exactly what Madison felt. It happened at about that age to me, too."

It happened. You might be wondering what is the *it* to which this Black woman is referring. To help you understand the *it*, I will take you into an extraordinary and vulnerable moment between Madison, her dad, her Aunt Charlie, and myself. In this moment, Madison shared things with us that I was not prepared to hear from my then 10-year-old, but I am so glad she did.

On a warm June day, just a few days shy of Madison's 11th birthday, Madison and I found ourselves nestled on the living room couch, sharing a heart-to-heart conversation. We had started talking about her upcoming birthday party but had begun to reflect over her last year in elementary school. Madison recounted the highs and lows of her elementary school journey, our chat flowed seamlessly, much like the countless others we'd had. But then, something shifted in her tone. Seemingly out of nowhere, Madison's eyes welled up with tears, and her voice quivered as she uttered the words that would forever change the way I saw her world: "I just don't understand why everyone was so mean to me. No one liked me. I don't know what I did. I don't know why." It was a sudden revelation, but it was the culmination of a year's worth of silent suffering for Madison.

As Madison courageously unraveled her feelings and began to share anecdotes I had never heard before, it became clear that she had ventured into a world unique to the experience of being a Black girl. When she recounted an incident from a school dance, where white female students deliberately excluded her, shunning her from a final group moment, the floodgates of emotion burst open. She couldn't fathom why they were so cruel, so incredibly heartless. But this was not an isolated incident. Madison revealed several instances of feeling excluded, ignored, and even ridiculed by her peers—for her hair, for the way she spoke. Each story was a dagger to my heart, hearing how she had internalized these painful experiences and questioned her own worth. What made it even more heart-wrenching was that sometimes, these injustices played out right under the watchful eyes of adults. She talked about subtle differences she noticed in how some adults talked to her and how some adults seemed to change their tone when they spoke to her. Madison had stopped seeking adult intervention because she believed they would utter the same dismissive phrases: "Don't be so sensitive; just ignore them. . . ." She felt like her emotions were constantly invalidated, causing her to feel even more isolated and misunderstood. It was disheartening to see Madison lose faith in the support system that should have protected her, as she desperately longed for someone to truly understand and address the hurtful behavior she faced.

Hearing Madison's stories was heartbreaking, but it also revealed a critical truth: educators have a unique opportunity—and responsibility—to change this narrative. When teachers fail to notice, validate, or address these experiences, they inadvertently perpetuate the exclusion and harm Black girls like Madison face.

Madison's experiences were a wake-up call. They underscored the need for educators to proactively recognize and address the unique challenges Black girls navigate, ensuring their classrooms are safe, inclusive spaces. It isn't enough to ignore microaggressions or dismiss students' emotions; educators must act as advocates, using their authority to protect and uplift.

THEY SHOULD KNOW BETTER . . . RIGHT?

Madison's openness also prompted me to reflect on my own memories of her development—from birth to 10 years old. Like any parent, I recalled the smiles, laughter, and moments of discovery, when she learned to navigate the world around her. But

I also thought about the times when I may have unintentionally made her feel isolated, confused, or insecure. Parenting is incredibly challenging, and it's not always easy to get things right. There were moments when I struggled to fully understand Madison's needs and emotions, which led to frustration and mistakes. In reflecting on my own responses to her behavior, I thought about how often we, as educators and adults, find ourselves thinking, "They should know better" when faced with challenges. When we have those thoughts, we should pause to ask ourselves this: Are we holding Black girls to standards that are unrealistic for their age? Are we applying this expectation disproportionately, especially when a child's experiences—like Madison's—may shape their reactions differently?

As I reflected on my own behavior, I realized that moments like these aren't just individual lapses in judgment. They are rooted in a much larger, pervasive issue—the societal expectations placed on Black girls to behave, perform, and mature in ways that are not aligned with their development. For educators, this means we must examine how often we unconsciously apply these expectations in our classrooms. Do we apply them with all students, or do they appear more frequently with students who are Black, especially Black girls? When we look at Black girls, are we seeing their potential, their individuality, or are we seeing a set of assumptions about what they "should" know, based on their identities and the narratives about their place in the world?

In reflecting on my own experience with Madison, I understand that the impact of these assumptions isn't just felt in a single moment; it builds over time. For educators, this is where our responsibility lies. Instead of thinking Black girls should know better, we must ask ourselves: How can we create environments that advocate for Black girls' full humanity and girlhood? How can we offer understanding, empathy, and genuine support when they encounter difficulties or challenges in the classroom? Black girls, like all students, need to feel seen for who they truly are—not as lesser versions of their peers but as powerful beings with their own set of experiences. Educators must help them navigate the world, validate their emotions, and advocate for their well-being, not simply by doing the work for them, but by standing beside them and lifting them up.

THE ADULTIFICATION OF BLACK GIRLS

In our efforts to create an educational environment that truly supports Black girls, we must engage deeply with research that illuminates the realities they face. One critical study that speaks directly to the heart of this issue is the Georgetown Law Center on Poverty and Inequality's *Listening to Black Women and Girls: Lived Experiences of Adultification Bias*.[1] Through a combination of personal narratives and lived experiences, this study reveals the pervasive impact of adultification bias—the tendency to perceive Black girls as more mature, less innocent, and more responsible than their white peers—and the ways in which it shapes their experiences in educational settings and beyond.

The study provides compelling evidence of how adultification bias permeates the lives of Black girls, including their experiences in school. As the study highlights, Black girls are often held to higher standards than their peers, expected to act older, more responsible, and more capable than their years suggest. This expectation is not only unfair but harmful. One participant in the 17- to 23-year-old age group of the study shared, "And I think that since the society we live in is predominantly white . . . Black girls . . . are . . . outside of that like majority community. . . . We don't have the benefit also of having the empathy." This quote shows the emotional toll of adultification bias, which often manifests in higher expectations and harsher treatment of Black girls.

These higher expectations have tangible consequences in school. As we discussed in Chapter 1, research reveals that Black girls are disproportionately disciplined compared to their peers. Participants in the Georgetown study further suggest that this discipline is for behaviors that would be seen as less serious if exhibited by white students. One participant in the 17- to 23-year-old study group recalled, "[I] a Black girl . . . raised a different perspective—like . . . I remember saying, 'I'm not sure that I agree with that' or 'That doesn't make sense to me because . . . '—then it's like, because it's a Black girl raising the idea, now it's perceived with a tinge of just challenging authority." This illustrates how adultification bias not only leads to harsher discipline but also causes educators to misinterpret curiosity or self-advocacy as defiance, placing an unfair burden on Black girls to manage adult perceptions and exceptions at a young age.

For educators, this has critical implications. The study shows that the assumptions behind adultification bias can influence how we perceive and treat Black girls in the classroom. For example, when a Black girl misbehaves, we may be quicker to assume that she "should know better" due to societal expectations of maturity. This mindset leaves little room for understanding the complexities of her lived experiences and emotional development. One participant in the 13- to

17-year-old age group stated, "It's like, well, like I'm still a kid. Like I still mess up. But it just seem like you hit like a specific age like 13-years-old, and, anytime you do anything wrong, it's, 'Oh, you know better.' So you're gonna get like the worst punishment." This reflects how Black girls are often misinterpreted and their emotions dismissed or punished instead of being understood and supported.

Perhaps most concerning is the way adultification bias denies Black girls the space to be children. In the study, Black girls expressed the heavy burden of being expected to act older than their age, which stifled their ability to make mistakes, explore their identities, and grow from their experiences. Rather than being allowed to make mistakes, learn from them, and build resilience, Black girls often face the pressure of proving their maturity and competence at an early age. One participant in the 30+ age group noted, "I've watched, you know, teachers, and counselors, and these people get into these power struggles with these girls, because . . . it's like, 'I forget that she's 10, because when I asked her to do so and so . . . she responded like an adult. And so how do—how I treat this child like a child?" This sentiment is echoed by other participants who described how their childhoods were overshadowed by the pressures of adult expectations. "[T]hey're like, 'Oh, you should have known better; you should have known this and that.' So they're not even acting like we're children, you know what I mean—acknowledging that," said another participant.

As educators, we must recognize that these girls are first and foremost children who need time, space, and encouragement to grow and develop without the added pressure of adult expectations. As one participant in the 13- to 17-year-old age group noted, "I think that . . . adults in general need to . . . be reminded that Black young girls are still kids."

To create a supportive and inclusive learning environment for Black girls, educators must actively work to dismantle adultification bias. This means challenging the assumptions that lead to harsher treatment and unrealistic expectations, and instead offering Black girls the understanding, empathy, and space they need to navigate their developmental journey at their own pace. Only by doing so can we truly advocate for their humanity and support their growth as students and as individuals.

This study challenges us to be change agents in the lives of Black girls, to stand up against adultification bias, and to forge a path toward educational environments where every student, regardless of their race or gender, can flourish and reach their full potential.

WHERE TO BEGIN: DISMANTLING ADULTIFICATION BIAS

Practice 5—Advocate for Their Girlhood means developing working knowledge of how adultification bias impacts Black girls and then dismantling it. There are several places to begin dismantling adultification bias in education, but the first and perhaps most essential step is validating the experiences of Black girls. Validation acknowledges the emotions, perspectives, and lived experiences of Black girls without judgment or dismissal. It is an intentional act of affirming their humanity and countering the bias that often invalidates or diminishes their feelings. Validating experiences means creating a space where Black girls feel heard, valued, and supported. It involves listening actively, reframing responses, and choosing words that affirm rather than dismiss. Validation does not mean excusing behavior or agreeing with everything a student says, but rather, it is about recognizing their perspective as legitimate and worth understanding.

Here are actionable strategies for practicing validation:

- **Listen Actively**
  - **What You Can Do**: Pause and give your full attention when a Black girl is sharing her feelings or concerns. Avoid interrupting or immediately offering solutions.
  - **Sample Statement**: "I hear you, and I appreciate your sharing this with me. Let's talk about how we can address it."

- **Acknowledge Emotions**
  - **What You Can Do**: Reflect back the emotions the student might be feeling to show you understand.
  - **Sample Statement**: "It sounds like you're feeling frustrated. That's completely valid, and I'm here to help figure this out."

- **Avoid Minimization**
  - **What You Can Do**: Resist the urge to downplay their feelings or tell them "it's not a big deal." Instead, take their concerns seriously.
  - **Sample Statement**: "I can see why this feels unfair to you. Let's explore what we can do together."

- **Invite Their Perspective**
  - **What You Can Do**: Encourage Black girls to share their perspectives, even in moments of conflict, and respond with curiosity rather than judgment.

○ **Sample Statement**: "Help me understand how you're seeing this situation. I want to make sure I get it right."

WHY IT MATTERS

Validating the experiences of Black girls counters the harmful effects of adultification bias by showing them that their feelings and perspectives are important. This practice builds trust, encourages open communication, and allows students to feel safe and supported in their learning environment. Most importantly, it reinforces the idea that Black girls deserve the same grace, empathy, and understanding afforded to all children.

UNDERSTANDING THE DEVELOPING MIND

Advocating for Black girls' girlhood also requires an understanding of the neuroscience of the developing mind. Neuroscience provides a valuable lens through which we can observe these developing minds in young people, particularly during the middle school years. The adolescent brain is still growing, and the emotional and cognitive processes of young people—particularly during stressful situations—are shaped by this ongoing development. Their brains are like a canvas, still being painted, and their emotions and decision-making skills are a work in progress. Understanding this is crucial to breaking down the biases that persist in our society. Let's explore how this science shapes the experiences of young Black girls. Armed with this knowledge, we can challenge biases and ensure age-appropriate interactions that support their growth.

Adolescence is a critical developmental phase marked by significant neurological changes, particularly in the prefrontal cortex. This brain region, responsible for impulse control, decision-making, and assessing consequences, matures gradually throughout adolescence and into early adulthood.[2] During this time, the adolescent brain remains highly plastic, making it adaptable yet vulnerable to cognitive overload and environmental influences.[3]

These changes emphasize the importance of structured classroom routines and predictable transitions to support students' developing executive functions. As teachers design lessons, creating intentional mental transitions can help students avoid cognitive overload, which occurs when working memory is overwhelmed.[4] If such transitions are absent, students may rely on less-developed brain regions, leading to behaviors that may not align with educators' expectations. This aligns with the principle that an adolescent's prefrontal cortex is not yet fully equipped to regulate behavior without external scaffolding.[5]

When working with teachers, instructional coaches, and administrators, I emphasize the need for classroom routines that align with the cognitive and neurological realities of adolescent learners. A frequent reminder I provide is *If educators do not design transitions to mitigate cognitive overload, students will create their own mental transitions—often influenced by their immature prefrontal cortex—which may not lead to the desired classroom outcomes.* We typically laugh a little bit as we consider the potential for innocent silliness resulting from students creating their own mental transitions. However, the reality is that without intentional and structured transitions, students may struggle to effectively shift their focus and retain information. This highlights the importance of teachers proactively incorporating transitional strategies into their teaching practices. Creating predictable and consistent routines for transitions in classrooms and lessons can optimize student learning. By providing this lens into the minds of our adolescent students, educators can be empowered to guide their students' prefrontal cortex development during these transitions, ultimately leading to desired outcomes.

Understanding the behaviors typically exhibited by middle school adolescents is key to creating effective classroom routines and strategies. The following chart provides an overview of common developmental behaviors in this age group, offering insight into how these behaviors manifest during this critical period of cognitive and emotional growth.

BEHAVIOR	EXPLANATION	HOW EDUCATORS MIGHT ADDRESS IT
Increased emotional sensitivity	Adolescents experience heightened emotions, which may lead to stronger reactions to peer interactions and classroom events.	Use regular emotional check-ins and mindfulness to help manage emotions.[6]
Desire for independence	Middle school students begin to seek more independence, especially from authority figures, while still needing guidance.	Offer choice and responsibility in activities to promote independence.[7]
Exploring self-identity	Adolescents begin to focus more on their sense of self, exploring different interests, roles, and beliefs.	Provide opportunities for self-expression through projects.[8]

(Continued)

BEHAVIOR	EXPLANATION	HOW EDUCATORS MIGHT ADDRESS IT
Social comparison	Peer relationships become central; students often compare themselves to others in terms of appearance, skills, and status.	Foster positive peer interactions and teamwork.[9]
Impulsivity and risk-taking	Due to the ongoing development of the prefrontal cortex, adolescents may act impulsively without fully considering consequences.	Create clear routines with steps for decision-making.[10]
Need for peer validation	Peer approval and group inclusion become highly significant, affecting decision-making and behaviors.	Build routines that encourage group support and self-validation.[11]
Variable attention span	Focus may fluctuate throughout the day due to changes in energy levels, interests, and emotional state.	Use structured transitions and movement breaks.[12]
Developing empathy	Adolescents become more aware of others' feelings and perspectives but may still struggle with regulating their emotional responses.	Encourage empathy-building activities like collaborative problem-solving.[13]

This chart highlights the key behaviors that can help inform classroom routines and transition strategies that are better suited to middle school students' developmental needs.

Adolescence is a complex period of brain development that unfolds gradually, particularly during middle school years, and is shaped by biological and environmental factors. The heightened emotional sensitivity and awareness of social dynamics often observed in adolescent girls are linked to changes in the limbic system, which matures earlier than the prefrontal cortex, the region responsible for impulse control and reasoning.[14] This mismatch can amplify emotions and peer-related conflicts while simultaneously fostering exploration of identity and interests, a hallmark of this developmental stage.[15]

NEURODIVERGENCE AND THE DEVELOPING MIND OF BLACK MIDDLE SCHOOL STUDENTS

The intersection of adolescence and neurodivergence creates a unique layer of complexity, especially for Black students. As we explore how to create truly inclusive environments for Black girls in middle school, it's critical to talk about neurodivergence—a topic that often gets overlooked when discussing educational equity. Think of this as another "warning label." If we do not also think about students who are neurodivergent when attending to the girlhood of Black girls, we can do much more harm than good. Recognizing the unique needs of students who are neurodivergent is not optional if we aim to foster environments that embrace and empower every learner.[16]

Here's the reality: neurodivergence—including conditions like ADHD, autism, and dyslexia—affects how students think, learn, and interact with the world around them.[17] For Black students, especially Black girls, who are already navigating the weight of societal stereotypes, being neurodivergent can present additional challenges. Studies have shown that Black girls are less likely to be identified and supported as neurodivergent and more likely to have their behaviors misinterpreted as defiance or disinterest.[18] See the disconnect? What might actually be a need for support gets misinterpreted as a problem to fix.

Take a moment to think about this in the context of the classroom or any learning environment. A student who is neurodivergent might struggle with transitions or sensory overload, which could manifest as a meltdown or withdrawal. Without an understanding of neurodivergence, educators might respond with punitive measures rather than support.[19] This creates an environment where the student doesn't feel seen, valued, or understood. And here's the issue: when that student is a Black girl, she's often subjected to harsher discipline than her peers, amplifying the harm caused by these misunderstandings.

To create truly inclusive spaces, educators must approach neurodivergence with the same cultural responsiveness we apply to race and identity. That means designing routines, lessons, and environments with flexibility, empathy, and awareness.[20] It's about shifting the mindset from "What's wrong with this student?" to "What does this student need?" Imagine how much more impactful our classrooms could be if we all adopted this approach.

Neurodivergent students, like all students, bring strengths and insights to the table. When we take the time to understand their needs—whether it's providing sensory breaks, using clear and consistent routines, or offering alternative ways to express understanding—we create spaces where they can thrive.[21] And when we pair this understanding with an awareness of how racism and genderism intersects with neurodivergence, we're not just teaching Black girls; we're empowering them. That's the goal, right?

The development of self-identity and personal passions during the middle school adolescent years period is universally experienced, transcending racial or ethnic boundaries. Research shows that adolescence is characterized by universal patterns of brain growth, including synaptic pruning and increased myelination, which shape cognitive and emotional functions across cultures.[22]This period of brain development in middle school and the years just before middle school is a universal experience that transcends racial boundaries. These processes provide the foundation for further maturation and are critical for navigating the challenges and opportunities of self-discovery during adolescence.[23]

So, how does understanding the neuroscience of adolescents help us cultivate better environments for Black girls? In a world where stereotypes from society perpetuate as norms that motivate and inform action, educators must be intentional about understanding what is and what is not developmentally appropriate for the behavior of adolescents and translate this understanding to how we respond to Black girls' behavior in the learning environment. Ultimately, this will lead to more supportive learning environments catering to their needs. Additionally, it helps educators recognize and address any biases or stereotypes that may influence their interactions with Black girls, fostering a more supportive and empowering educational experience for them.

Like all adolescents, Black girls navigate a whirlwind of emotions, test boundaries, and seek their identity. These behaviors often get misinterpreted as defiance or rebellion when they are essential components of healthy development. It's the brain's way of experimenting with autonomy and individuality. Furthermore, middle school is a time when social interactions become increasingly complex. Friendships, peer pressure, and a desire to fit in all play significant roles in the lives of these young girls. As educators, recognizing that these behaviors and emotions are part of the normal developmental process is pivotal. It allows us to provide a supportive and empathetic environment for Black girls in middle school. By acknowledging these factors and integrating them into our transformative practices, we can better address the needs of our young Black students and foster a more inclusive and positive educational space for all.

WHERE TO BEGIN: RE-DRESSING EXPECTATIONS

Practice 5—Advocate for Their Girlhood means not only dismantling adultification bias but also actively replacing unrealistic and developmentally inappropriate expectations with ones that honor the normal, healthy development of Black girls.

Re-dressing expectations requires understanding the behaviors and emotions that are typical for adolescents, recognizing how these can be misinterpreted through biased lenses, and making intentional shifts to set expectations that reflect developmental norms.

Black girls, like all adolescents, are navigating a period of significant growth and self-discovery. Behaviors such as testing boundaries, expressing emotions intensely, or seeking independence are not acts of rebellion but essential parts of their journey to autonomy and self-identity. Yet, adultification bias often warps perceptions of these behaviors, leading to punitive responses instead of supportive guidance.

Re-dressing expectations means reframing how educators perceive and respond to Black girls' behavior. It involves fostering an environment where their developmental needs are understood and met with empathy and support rather than judgment or unrealistic demands.

HOW EDUCATORS CAN RE-DRESS EXPECTATIONS

Here are actionable strategies for aligning expectations with developmental realities:

- Normalize Developmental Behaviors
  - **What You Can Do**: Educate yourself and your staff about the typical behaviors and emotional shifts of adolescence. Approach these behaviors with curiosity rather than frustration.
  - **Sample Statement**: "It's completely normal to feel this way at your age. Let's talk about how we can work through it together."

- Set Clear, Developmentally Appropriate Boundaries
  - **What You Can Do**: Establish guidelines that reflect an understanding of adolescents' needs for autonomy and structure. Ensure consequences are equitable and not disproportionately harsh for Black girls.
  - **Sample Statement**: "We all make mistakes—it's part of learning. Here's how we can use this moment as a learning opportunity."

- Celebrate Individuality and Growth
  - **What You Can Do**: Encourage Black girls to embrace their individuality and recognize their strengths while helping them navigate the challenges of adolescence.

- ○ **Sample Statement**: "I see so many strengths within you. Let's figure out how we can use your talents to shine even brighter."
- **Provide Opportunities for Self-reflection and Expression**
  - ○ **What You Can Do**: Create spaces where Black girls can process their emotions, set goals, and express their thoughts without fear of judgment.
  - ○ **Sample Statement**: "How do you feel about what happened? Let's think about what you might do differently next time."

WHY IT MATTERS

Re-dressing expectations ensures that Black girls are seen and supported as children navigating a critical stage of growth. When educators adopt developmentally appropriate expectations, it reduces the risk of punitive responses and creates a safer, more supportive learning environment. It also communicates to Black girls that their growth, mistakes, and successes are valid and worthy of encouragement, not condemnation.

Real change requires a deeper understanding of Black girls' challenges. It means recognizing that they bear the weight of adultification bias and its consequences from a young age. This expectation that they should "know better" robs them of their childhood and restricts their development, self-discovery, and exploration.

As an educator, I've learned that to challenge this notion effectively, we must take a multifaceted approach. We must foster empathy and understanding, encouraging conversations with Black girls that lead to a more informed perspective. It is vital to acknowledge that Black girls, like all young people, are still learning about the world around them. They are not born with an inherent understanding of societal complexities, and it is unjust to expect them to navigate these issues effortlessly. Moreover, we must focus on proactive steps to create a more inclusive and equitable environment for Black girls in our educational institutions. This means revising policies, providing mentorship and support networks, and ensuring that educators are equipped with the tools and knowledge to address the unique needs of Black girls. It requires curricula that reflect their experiences and a commitment to eradicating racial and gender biases.

In my role as an advocate, I've also come to understand the importance of amplifying the voices of Black girls themselves. By listening to their experiences, concerns, and aspirations, we can gain a deeper insight into their challenges and the support they require. Their perspectives should guide our efforts, ensuring that our solutions are informed by their needs and aspirations. The journey from saying, "You should know better" to advocating for the fair chances and equitable treatment of Black girls in our educational system is profound and transformative. It's about recognizing their unique struggles and challenges and working together to dismantle the systemic biases that have held them back for far too long. By doing so, we empower Black girls to reach their full potential and contribute to a more just and inclusive society for all.

In the Middle

Advocate for Their Girlhood

In this section, take a moment to reflect on the information and strategies shared throughout the chapter on **dismantling adultification bias** and **re-dressing expectations**. These two strategies are vital steps in implementing **Practice 5—Advocate for Their Girlhood** and ensuring Black girls are supported in their growth, humanity, and potential.

Consider how these approaches can help create a learning environment where Black girls feel seen, valued, and empowered. Think about how you can begin incorporating these strategies into your everyday interactions and classroom culture. This reflection is an opportunity to identify practical, intentional steps toward fostering an inclusive and affirming environment for Black girls, where they can thrive academically, socially, and emotionally.

REFLECTION TASK

Take a moment to reflect on the following questions. Choose one or all three to think deeply about. These questions are designed to help you connect the strategies in this chapter to your work and identify areas for growth. There are no right or wrong answers—just an opportunity to explore your thoughts and plan actionable next steps.

1. **How can you validate the experiences of Black girls in your setting?** Reflect on the strategies for dismantling adultification bias. Which approach—such as active listening, acknowledging emotions, or avoiding minimization—feels most impactful for your students? How can you make it a regular part of your practice?

   _____

   _____

   _____

2. **How can you re-dress expectations to better align with adolescent development?** Think about how you currently set expectations for Black girls. Are they developmentally appropriate? What shifts could you make to celebrate individuality, normalize healthy adolescent behaviors, and foster their growth?

   _____

   _____

   _____

3. **Where do you see the greatest opportunity for growth in your practice?** Consider both steps—dismantling adultification bias and re-dressing expectations. Which area do you feel needs the most attention in your environment? What is one small, actionable change you can make today to better advocate for the girlhood of Black students?

_____

_____

_____

The Weight of Expectations

Jada's Story

Jada's bright smile and infectious laughter lit up every room she entered. At 12 years old, her boundless energy and playful spirit were the essence of childhood—a joy to be cherished. One afternoon, during a lively classroom activity, Jada's excitement got the better of her, and she accidentally knocked over a stack of books. The thud echoed across the room, followed by a brief pause as everyone turned toward the source of the commotion.

Her teacher's reaction came swiftly. Unlike the gentle reminders or light-hearted comments that usually followed similar mishaps with her peers, Jada was met with a stern tone and a piercing look of disapproval. The warmth in the room seemed to dissipate as Jada's shoulders slumped under the weight of expectations she didn't fully understand. It wasn't the first time she had felt this way, as if the unspoken rules for her were somehow different—harsher, less forgiving.

Jada sat quietly for the rest of the lesson, her mind replaying the incident. She couldn't articulate it yet, but this moment was a window into a pattern she would come to recognize: a burden placed upon her, asking her to be more mature, more composed, more than a child. This was adultification bias in action, a subtle but powerful force that shifted how others saw her and, ultimately, how she saw herself.

For educators, Jada's story is a reminder and a call to action. The quiet moments of inequity, like the one she experienced, carry lasting weight. They reveal the necessity of recognizing and dismantling biases that disproportionately affect Black girls. Every child deserves the grace to stumble, to laugh, to knock over a stack of books without it becoming a lesson in undue responsibility. And in doing so, educators can ensure their classrooms are places of growth, understanding, and joy for every child, just as they should be.

NOTES

1. Blake, J. J., & Epstein, R. (2017). *Listening to Black women and girls: Lived experiences of adultification bias.* Georgetown Law Center on Poverty and Inequality.

2. Blakemore, S. J., & Choudhury, S. (2006). Development of the adolescent brain: Implications for executive function and social cognition. *Journal of Child Psychology and Psychiatry, 47*(3), 296–312.

3. Johnson, M. H., Grossmann, T., & Kadosh, K. C. (2009). Mapping functional brain development: Building a social brain through interactive specialization. *Developmental Psychology, 45*(1), 151–159.

4. Sweller, J. (1988). Cognitive load during problem solving: Effects on learning. *Cognitive Science, 12*(2), 257–285.

5. Casey, B. J., Jones, R. M., & Hare, T. A. (2008). The adolescent brain. *Annals of the New York Academy of Sciences, 1124*(1), 111–126.

6. Roeser, R. W., Eccles, J. S., & Sameroff, A. J. (2003). *School as a context of early adolescent development.* Jossey-Bass.

7. Steinberg, L., & Morris, A. S. (2001). Adolescent development. *Annual Review of Psychology, 52,* 83–110.

8. Erikson, E. H. (1968). *Identity: Youth and crisis.* Norton.

9. Harter, S. (2012). *The construction of the self.* Guilford Press.

10. Casey, B. J., Jones, R. M., & Hare, T. A. (2008). The adolescent brain. Annals of the New York Academy of Sciences, 1124(1), 111–126.

11. Brown, B. B. (2004). Adolescents' relationships with peers. In *Handbook of adolescent psychology* (2nd ed.). Wiley.

12. Jensen, E. (2005). *Teaching with the brain in mind.* ASCD.

13. Goleman, D. (2006). Emotional intelligence. Bantam Books.

14. Blakemore, S. J. (2012). Imaging brain development: The adolescent brain. *NeuroImage, 61*(2), 397–406.

15. Crone, E. A., & Dahl, R. E. (2012). Understanding adolescence as a period of social-affective engagement and goal flexibility. *Nature Reviews Neuroscience, 13*(9), 636–650.

16. Collins, K., Ferri, B. A., & Connor, D. J. (2016). *DisCrit expanded: Disability studies and critical race theory in education.* Teachers College Press.

17. Singer, J. (1999). *Why can't you be normal for once in your life? From a "problem with no name" to the emergence of a new category of difference.* In M. Corker & S. French (Eds.), *Disability discourse.* Open University Press.

18. Crenshaw, K., Ocen, P., & Nanda, J. (2015). *Black girls matter: Pushed out, overpoliced and underprotected.* African American Policy Forum.

19. Gilliam, W. S., Maupin, A. N., Reyes, C. R., Accavitti, M., & Shic, F. (2016). *Do early educators' implicit biases regarding sex and race relate to behavior expectations and recommendations of preschool expulsions and suspensions?* Yale Child Study Center.

20. Gay, G. (2018). *Culturally responsive teaching: Theory, research, and practice* (3rd ed.). Teachers College Press.

21. Rose, D. H., & Meyer, A. (2002). *Teaching every student in the digital age: Universal Design for Learning.* ASCD.

22. Casey et al. (2008).

23. Steinberg, L. (2014). *Age of opportunity: Lessons from the new science of adolescence.* Houghton Mifflin Harcourt.

CHAPTER 7

Partnering With Families and Communities

To create a transformative educational environment for Black girls, individual learning spaces and individual adults must serve as the starting point—but not the endpoint. True transformation requires systemic change that extends across entire schools, districts, and community organizations and involves several adult changemakers. By adopting a cohesive, collaborative approach, we can build environments where Black girls are not just supported but celebrated. Broader, wide-scale actions can ignite systemic change and sustain meaningful progress for Black girls.

THE NECESSITY OF SYSTEMIC CHANGE

Systemic change acknowledges that individual efforts, while impactful, are limited if larger structures remain unresponsive to the needs of Black girls. Disparities in disciplinary practices and the absence of culturally affirming curricula are not isolated issues—they are systemic ones. Transforming these entrenched challenges requires intentionality, collaboration, and a framework for sustained action.

The work begins with recognizing the interconnectedness of policies, practices, and beliefs. It requires all stakeholders—educators, administrators, policymakers, and community leaders—to operate with a shared vision and commitment to equity. Through this collective effort, we can dismantle barriers and create ecosystems that foster opportunity, belonging, and success for Black girls.

SCALING THE BELIEF FRAMEWORK

To ensure systemic efforts are intentional and measurable, the **BELIEF framework** provides a practical roadmap for scaling transformative practices across classrooms, schools, districts, and community organizations. First introduced in the Introduction, let's revisit its components with a systemic lens:

- **B – Begin With Belief**

  At the foundation of systemic change is the unwavering belief in the brilliance, resilience, and humanity of Black girls. School, district, and organizational leaders must commit to fostering an organizational culture that centers these beliefs. Professional development initiatives should prioritize equity-focused training, helping educators and administrators confront and dismantle implicit biases. Community organizations can align their missions to amplify the voices and experiences of Black girls, ensuring every action reflects this foundational belief.

- **E – Envision Their Futures**

  Schools and districts must collaboratively define a clear, ambitious vision for Black girls' futures. This vision should encompass academic achievement, social-emotional growth, and preparation for lifelong success. Engage Black girls, their families, and community stakeholders in co-creating this vision. Their insights ensure that goals are relevant, empowering, and culturally affirming. Community organizations can partner with schools to provide mentorship, internships, and leadership opportunities that align with these aspirations.

- **L – Leverage Data**

  Systemic change requires the strategic use of data. Schools and districts must gather and analyze disaggregated data on academic outcomes, discipline rates, attendance, and course enrollment to uncover inequities and track progress. Listening sessions with Black girls and their families can provide critical anecdotal data, offering deeper context and understanding. Community organizations can contribute by sharing insights from their work, fostering a more holistic view of Black girls' experiences.

- **I – Implement Your Practices**

  Translating belief and vision into action demands consistent and widespread implementation of evidence-based practices.

Schools can adopt culturally responsive teaching, revise disciplinary policies, and create affinity groups for Black girls. Districts can embed equity goals into strategic plans, ensuring accountability at all levels. Community organizations can offer culturally relevant programming, mentorship, and advocacy to complement school-based efforts.

- **E – Evaluate Your Efforts**

  Evaluation is key to understanding the effectiveness of systemic initiatives. Schools and districts should regularly assess the impact of their policies and practices on Black girls, using both quantitative and qualitative data. Community partners can contribute by conducting independent evaluations of their programs, providing critical feedback for continuous improvement.

- **F – Fortify Your Approaches**

  Sustaining systemic change requires ongoing reflection and adaptation. Schools and districts should create equity committees that meet regularly to review progress and recommend adjustments. Community organizations can host annual forums, bringing together stakeholders to celebrate successes and identify areas for growth. By fortifying these approaches, we ensure that efforts remain dynamic and responsive to the evolving needs of Black girls.

PARTNERING WITH FAMILIES AND COMMUNITIES: EXPANDING HER SUPPORT NETWORK

Systemic change cannot occur in isolation. It requires meaningful partnerships with families and community organizations. Black girls thrive when they are surrounded by a robust network of support that includes educators, family members, and community leaders who share a commitment to their success.

ENGAGING FAMILIES

Families are invaluable allies in the effort to support Black girls. Schools and districts must create spaces where families feel welcomed, valued, and heard. Strategies for family engagement include the following:

- Hosting culturally relevant family nights that celebrate Black culture and provide resources for academic and social-emotional support

- Creating family advisory councils to involve parents and caregivers in decision-making processes
- Establishing regular communication channels that share updates on Black girls' progress and invite feedback from families

By building trust and fostering collaboration, schools can strengthen the connection between home and school, ensuring Black girls receive consistent support in all areas of their lives.

PARTNERING WITH COMMUNITY ORGANIZATIONS

Community organizations play a crucial role in extending support beyond the school walls. They can offer programs and services that complement school-based efforts, such as the following:

- Mentorship programs that connect Black girls with role models who reflect their identities and aspirations
- Leadership development initiatives that build confidence, resilience, and advocacy skills
- Enrichment opportunities, such as STEM camps, arts programs, and community service projects, that broaden Black girls' horizons and expose them to new possibilities

To maximize impact, schools and districts should formalize partnerships with community organizations, aligning goals and coordinating efforts to create a seamless support network for Black girls.

BUILDING A CULTURE OF COLLECTIVE RESPONSIBILITY

Systemic change demands a culture of collective responsibility, where all stakeholders—educators, administrators, families, and community members—recognize their role in creating equitable opportunities for Black girls. This culture is built on shared accountability, open communication, and a commitment to continuous improvement.

School districts can lead the way by

- embedding equity goals into their mission statements and strategic plans;

- providing ongoing professional development focused on culturally responsive practices and equity leadership; and

- celebrating successes, sharing stories of Black girls' achievements to inspire and sustain momentum.

Community organizations can amplify these efforts by

- advocating for policy changes that promote equity and inclusion;

- offering scholarships, grants, and other resources to support Black girls' academic and personal growth; and

- hosting public events that highlight the importance of systemic change and galvanize community support.

A VISION FOR THE FUTURE

Systemic change for Black girls is not a destination but a journey. By leveraging the BELIEF framework, forging strong partnerships, and fostering a culture of collective responsibility, we can create ecosystems that empower Black girls to thrive. The work ahead is challenging, but the rewards are immeasurable.

Vignette

A Journey of Support and Growth

In a middle school, a group of six Black girls in the eighth grade were caught in the middle of adolescent drama—conflicts among themselves and with other students. These girls, who had varying academic performance levels, were navigating the complicated transition from childhood to teenagehood. They each faced personal challenges in managing relationships and coping with adversity, yet all shared a common need: a space to discuss and process their experiences in a supportive, understanding environment.

Recognizing the importance of addressing both the social-emotional and academic needs of these students, their counselor, Mrs. Marshall, began to explore ways to offer them meaningful support. The challenges they faced weren't just typical middle school drama. The girls'

(Continued)

(Continued)

interpersonal struggles reflected deeper issues related to self-expression, identity, and how they related to one another within the larger school culture.

B – Begin With Belief

Mrs. Marshall understood that the foundation of any effort must be grounded in an unwavering belief in the potential of these girls. Despite the challenges they faced, she recognized that each girl was capable of success. This belief was central to the effort, ensuring that the students' unique experiences and needs were approached with empathy and respect.

E – Envision Their Futures

With a deep commitment to their growth, Mrs. Marshall envisioned a future where these girls could confidently navigate the challenges of adolescence, equipped with the tools to manage conflicts, understand their worth, and support each other in constructive ways. It was clear that the girls needed a safe space to express themselves, share their challenges, and develop the social-emotional skills to build stronger relationships.

L – Leverage Data

To better understand the root causes of these struggles, Mrs. Marshall reviewed a variety of data, including attendance records, discipline referrals, and academic performance, while also gathering direct feedback from the girls themselves. The data revealed that many of the conflicts stemmed from struggles with self-identity, peer pressure, and the stress of balancing academic and social challenges. The girls voiced that they felt isolated at times and lacked a space to discuss their experiences. This insight highlighted the need for a more structured, supportive environment where the girls could reflect on their emotions, practice healthy communication, and build resilience.

I – Implement Your Practices

With this information, Mrs. Marshall collaborated with a Black female teacher, who had built strong relationships with the girls, to create a new support group—a dedicated affinity group for the six girls—designed to meet during the school's Advisory time. This time, already set aside for social-emotional and academic development, provided the perfect opportunity to offer a space where the girls could reflect, share, and grow together. The group was led by the teacher, Mrs. Hawkins, who understood their unique needs and created a culturally responsive space for the girls.

The group's activities included discussions about handling peer pressure, expressing emotions, and maintaining strong self-identity. The students worked on skills like conflict resolution, active listening, and developing mutual support networks. They learned how to navigate difficult conversations with friends and how to approach misunderstandings constructively. Throughout their time together, the girls bonded, learning how to support one another in ways that went beyond the typical drama and conflict.

E – Evaluate Your Efforts

After several weeks of meetings, feedback was gathered from the girls about their experience. Many of the girls shared that they felt more connected to each other and better equipped to handle conflicts.

Teachers also noticed a change: there were fewer disruptions, and the girls seemed more engaged and confident in their academic work. Some of the girls even reported improved attendance, indicating that they felt more supported and connected to the school community.

The group's success wasn't just about resolving conflicts but also about fostering a sense of belonging. By giving these girls a platform to voice their concerns and learn strategies for managing adversity, the group meetings empowered them to navigate their social worlds with greater resilience.

F – Fortify Your Approaches

Encouraged by the positive outcomes, Mrs. Marshall and Mrs. Hawkins decided to expand the group's impact by providing the girls with leadership opportunities throughout the building. They allowed the students to visit other Advisory classes, including sixth-grade classrooms, where they served as mentors to younger female students. Over time, the group adapted to the changing needs of the students, continuously refining their discussions and activities to ensure they remained relevant and impactful.

By applying the BELIEF framework, the counselor was able to create a space where these six girls felt seen, heard, and supported. The affinity group provided a consistent, culturally responsive environment for them to address their social-emotional needs, deepen their self-awareness, and build the skills to navigate challenges. Through this intentional and inclusive approach, the girls were not only able to manage conflict more effectively but also develop stronger relationships with each other, contributing to a more positive and supportive school climate.

Conclusion

Transforming Learning for Black Girls

In *Black Girl in the Middle: Five Transformative Practices to Make School Better for Black Girls*, we have been challenged through reflection, building, and advocacy, all centered around transformative practices that hold the power to create a brighter, more inclusive future for Black girls in educational settings. Through these pages, we have explored five practices that have consistently and vividly demonstrated their ability to uplift, empower, and enrich the lives of Black girls in school.

Retracing our steps through the preceding chapters reveals the intricate tapestry of experiences that define Black girls' lives and the hope that exists within them. Throughout our exploration, we have witnessed the resilience and strength that Black girls possess, defying societal expectations and breaking barriers. Now, armed with this understanding, we are ready to pursue even deeper efforts to empower these young individuals to reach their full potential and to create a more inclusive future for all.

THE JOURNEY OF TRANSFORMATION

In our journey through the pages of *Black Girl in the Middle*, we've delved into the complex, often overlooked world of Black girls in our educational system. We've explored their unique challenges and uncovered their remarkable potential. This journey has been one of discovery, a call to action to critically examine our beliefs, practices, and systems.

Here's the truth: systemic change for Black girls is not an easy path, but it is a necessary one. Their brilliance, resilience, and humanity deserve nothing less. Yet, to truly transform learning environments, we must remain vigilant. Without intentionality, well-meaning practices can inadvertently reinforce harmful systems.

To navigate this transformative work effectively, let us revisit the five practices that have guided us:

- **Practice One—Identify Your Beliefs**
  - What do you believe about the social-emotional and academic presence of Black girls? How do your actions communicate this belief?

- **Practice Two—Plant the SEAD**
  - How do you support the social-emotional and academic growth of Black girls? Are your actions intentional in fostering both their emotional well-being and academic success?

- **Practice Three—Listen With Compassion**
  - How do you demonstrate compassionate listening? Are you listening to what they say, how they say it, and what they are really communicating?

- **Practice Four—Encourage Positive Self-Talk**
  - When and how do you encourage positive self-talk? Are you intentional about fostering self-affirming thoughts and reinforcing their sense of worth?

- **Practice Five—Advocate for Their Girlhood**
  - How do you respond to Black girls academically and socially? Do you engage with Black girls in age-appropriate ways, honoring their developmental stage and individuality?

Each of these practices represents a steppingstone on the journey toward creating a school culture that not only includes but celebrates Black girls. By revisiting these practices regularly, measuring outcomes, and incorporating feedback, educators and leaders can ensure that these foundations remain strong and relevant.

A CALL TO ACTION

This book, as you've discovered, shares five transformative practices that hold the power to revolutionize the learning experiences of Black girls. These practices are not just ideas but keys to a more inclusive, empowering, and equitable education. They embody a promise to make learning better for Black girls in schools.

As we conclude this journey, let it not be the end but the beginning of a movement. Let the knowledge within these pages fuel your passion to transform learning for Black girls. Let these five transformative practices guide you, illuminating the path toward a more inclusive, equitable, and empowering educational system.

You hold the promise of change, the key to a brighter future for Black girls in the middle. Together, we can create an educational landscape that respects their identities, nurtures their potential, and empowers them to reach for the stars. As we stride into the future, remember that it's not only Black girls who benefit from our collective efforts; society as a whole reaps the rewards of their achievements. The empowerment of Black girls means a more diverse, inclusive, and enlightened world for us all.

Thank you for joining me on this transformative journey. May your efforts continue to light the path toward a brighter, more equitable future for Black girls and, by extension, the world they will lead.

Index

CORWIN

To help every educator help every student

We believe   that every single student
               deserves a great education

We believe   that knowing our impact is both
               a privilege and a responsibility

We believe   that a fair, stable, and thriving
               society is built on education